T0214624

Foundations of ARM64 Linux Debugging, Disassembling, and Reversing

Analyze Code, Understand Stack Memory Usage, and Reconstruct Original C/C++ Code with ARM64

Dmitry Vostokov

Apress®

Foundations of ARM64 Linux Debugging, Disassembling, and Reversing:
Analyze Code, Understand Stack Memory Usage, and Reconstruct Original
C/C++ Code with ARM64

Dmitry Vostokov
Dublin, Ireland

ISBN-13 (pbk): 978-1-4842-9081-1   ISBN-13 (electronic): 978-1-4842-9082-8
https://doi.org/10.1007/978-1-4842-9082-8

Managing Director, Apress Media LLC: Welmoed Spahr
Acquisitions Editor: Celestin Suresh John
Development Editor: James Markham
Coordinating Editor: Mark Powers

Cover designed by eStudioCalamar

Cover image by Susan Wilkinson on Unsplash (www.unsplash.com)

Distributed to the book trade worldwide by Apress Media, LLC, 1 New York Plaza, New York, NY 10004, U.S.A. Phone 1-800-SPRINGER, fax (201) 348-4505, e-mail orders-ny@springer-sbm.com, or visit www.springeronline.com. Apress Media, LLC is a California LLC and the sole member (owner) is Springer Science + Business Media Finance Inc (SSBM Finance Inc). SSBM Finance Inc is a **Delaware** corporation.

For information on translations, please e-mail booktranslations@springernature.com; for reprint, paperback, or audio rights, please e-mail bookpermissions@springernature.com.

Apress titles may be purchased in bulk for academic, corporate, or promotional use. eBook versions and licenses are also available for most titles. For more information, reference our Print and eBook Bulk Sales web page at http://www.apress.com/bulk-sales.

Any source code or other supplementary material referenced by the author in this book is available to readers on GitHub (https://github.com/Apress). For more detailed information, please visit http://www.apress.com/source-code.

Printed on acid-free paper

Table of Contents

About the Author

 **Dmitry Vostokov** is an internationally recognized expert, speaker, educator, scientist, and author. He is the founder of the pattern-oriented software diagnostics, forensics, and prognostics discipline and Software Diagnostics Institute (DA+TA: DumpAnalysis. org + TraceAnalysis.org). Vostokov has also authored more than 50 books on software diagnostics, anomaly detection and analysis, software and memory forensics, root cause analysis and problem solving, memory dump analysis, debugging, software trace and log analysis, reverse engineering, and malware analysis. He has more than 25 years of experience in software architecture, design, development, and maintenance in various industries, including leadership, technical, and people management roles. Dmitry also founded Syndromatix, Anolog. io, BriteTrace, DiaThings, Logtellect, OpenTask Iterative and Incremental Publishing (OpenTask.com), Software Diagnostics Technology and Services (former Memory Dump Analysis Services; PatternDiagnostics. com), and Software Prognostics. In his spare time, he presents various topics on Debugging TV and explores Software Narratology, its further development as Narratology of Things and Diagnostics of Things (DoT), Software Pathology, and Quantum Software Diagnostics. His current areas of interest are theoretical software diagnostics and its mathematical and computer science foundations, application of formal logic, artificial intelligence, machine learning and data mining to diagnostics and anomaly detection, software diagnostics engineering and diagnostics-driven

development, and diagnostics workflow and interaction. Recent areas of interest also include cloud native computing, security, automation, functional programming, and applications of category theory to software development and big data.

About the Technical Reviewer

 **Sundar Pandian** has more than three years of experience in embedded software development, including development of device drivers, middleware software, and application services for the infotainment system on the Android platform. He's also developed CAN protocol drivers for the automotive braking system on the Autosar platform.

He's developed software with C, C++, and Java and worked in the automotive, semiconductor, and telecom industries. He has a bachelor's in electronics and communication engineering. Currently, he serves as a firmware/middleware engineer for audio DSPs.

About the Technical Reviewer

Preface

The book covers topics ranging from ARM64 assembly language
instructions and writing programs in assembly language to pointers, live
debugging, and static binary analysis of compiled C and C++ code.

Diagnostics of core memory dumps, live and postmortem debugging
of Linux applications, services, and systems, memory forensics, malware,
and vulnerability analysis require an understanding of ARM64 assembly
language and how C and C++ compilers generate code, including
memory layout and pointers. This book is about background knowledge
and practical foundations that are needed to understand internal Linux
program structure and behavior, start working with the GDB debugger, and
use it for disassembly and reversing. It consists of practical step-by-step
exercises of increasing complexity with explanations and many diagrams,
including some necessary background topics.

By the end of the book, you will have a solid understanding of how
Linux C and C++ compilers generate binary code. In addition, you will be
able to analyze such code confidently, understand stack memory usage,
and reconstruct original C/C++ code.

The book will be useful for

- Software support and escalation engineers, cloud
  security engineers, SRE, and DevSecOps

- Software engineers coming from JVM background

- Software testers

- Engineers coming from non-Linux environments, for
  example, Windows or Mac OS X

- Engineers coming from non-ARM environments, for example, x86/x64

- Linux C/C++ software engineers without assembly language background

- Security researchers without assembly language background

- Beginners learning Linux software reverse engineering techniques

This book can also be used as an ARM64 assembly language and Linux debugging supplement for relevant undergraduate-level courses.

Source Code

All source code used in this book can be downloaded from github.com/apress/arm64-linux-debugging-disassembling-reversing.

CHAPTER 1

Memory, Registers, and Simple Arithmetic

Memory and Registers Inside an Idealized Computer

Computer memory consists of a sequence of memory cells, and each cell has a unique address (location). Every cell contains a "number." We refer to these "numbers" as contents at addresses (locations). Because memory access is slower than arithmetic instructions, there are so-called registers to speed up complex operations that require memory to store temporary results. We can also think about them as stand-alone memory cells. The name of a register is its address. Figure 1-1 illustrates this.

© Dmitry Vostokov 2023
D. Vostokov, *Foundations of ARM64 Linux Debugging, Disassembling, and Reversing*,
https://doi.org/10.1007/978-1-4842-9082-8_1

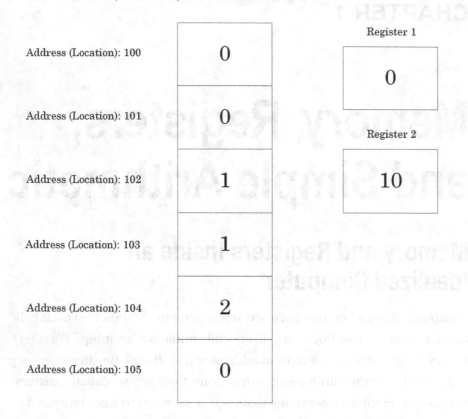

Figure 1-1. *Computer memory represented as a sequence of memory cells and locations*

Memory and Registers Inside ARM 64-Bit Computer

Here, addresses for memory locations containing integer values usually differ by four or eight, and we also show two registers called X0 and X1. The first halves of them are called W0 and W1 as shown in Figure 1-2.

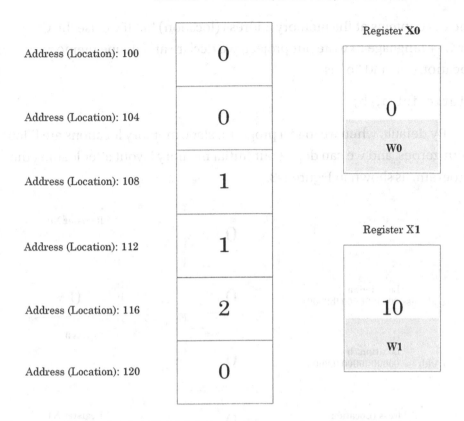

Figure 1-2. *Typical ARM 64-bit memory and register layout*

Because memory cells contain "numbers," we start with simple arithmetic and ask a processor to compute the sum of two numbers to see how memory and registers change their values.

"Arithmetic" Project: Memory Layout and Registers

For our project, we have two memory addresses (locations) that we call "a" and "b." We can think about "a" and "b" as names of their respective addresses (locations). Now we introduce a special notation where (a)

3

means contents at the memory address (location) "a." If we use the C or C++ language to write our project, we declare and define memory locations "a" and "b" as

```
static int a, b;
```

By default, when we load a program, static memory locations are filled with zeroes, and we can depict our initial memory layout after loading the program, as shown in Figure 1-3.

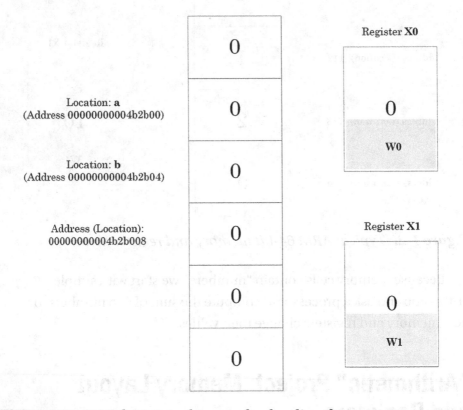

Figure 1-3. *Initial memory layout after loading the program*

"Arithmetic" Project: A Computer Program

We can think of a computer program as a sequence of instructions for the manipulation of contents of memory cells and registers. For example, addition operation: add the contents of memory cell №12 to the contents of memory cell №14. In our pseudo-code, we can write

```
[14] <- [14] + [12]
```

Our first program in pseudo-code is shown on the left of the table:

`[a] <- 1`	Here, we put assembly instructions corresponding to
`[b] <- 1`	pseudo-code.
`[b] <- [b] + [a]`	
`[a] <- [a] + 1`	
`[b] <- [b] * [a]`	

"<-" means moving (assigning) the new value to the contents of a memory location (address). "//" is a comment sign, and the rest of the line is a comment. "=" shows the current value at a memory location (address).

To remind, a code written in a high-level programming language is translated to a machine language by a compiler. However, the machine language can be readable if its digital codes are represented in some mnemonic system called assembly language. For example, **ADD X1, X1, #1** is increment by one of what is stored in the register memory cell X1.

"Arithmetic" Project: Assigning Numbers to Memory Locations

We remind that "a" means the location (address) of the memory cell, and it is also the name of the location (address) 00000000004b2b00 (see Figure 1-3). [a] means the contents (number) stored at the address "a."

5

If we use the C or C++ language, "a" is called "the variable a," and we write the assignment as

```
a = 1;
```

In ARM64 assembly language, we write several instructions for that:

```
adr x0, a
mov w1, #1
str w1, [x0]
```

In the GDB disassembly output, we may see the following code:

```
adrp    x0, 0x4b2000
add     x0, x0, #0xb00
mov     w1, #0x1
str     w1, [x0]
```

We show the translation of our pseudo-code into assembly language in the right column:

[a] <- 1	**// x0 = a**	**adr x0, a**
	// w1 = 1	**mov w1, #1**
	// [a] = 1	**str w1, [x0]**
[b] <- 1	**// x0 = b**	**adr x0, b**
	// w1 = 1	**mov w1, #1**
	// [b] = 1	**str w1, [x0]**
[b] <- [b] + [a]		
[a] <- [a] + 1		
[b] <- [b] * [a]		

adrp x0, 0x4b2000, and subsequent add x0, x0, #0xb00 is how the compiler generates code to calculate the address "a" instead of specifying it directly. Such code is required for addressing large regions of memory, and the compiler uses it even for smaller regions where just one adr instruction is sufficient.

Literal constants have the # prefix, for example, #0x1. The 0x prefix means the following number is hexadecimal. We explain such numbers in Chapter 3. Please also notice that the movement direction is the same in both the disassembly output and the pseudo-code: from right to left (except for the str instruction).

After executing the first three assembly language instructions, we have the memory layout shown in Figure 1-4A.

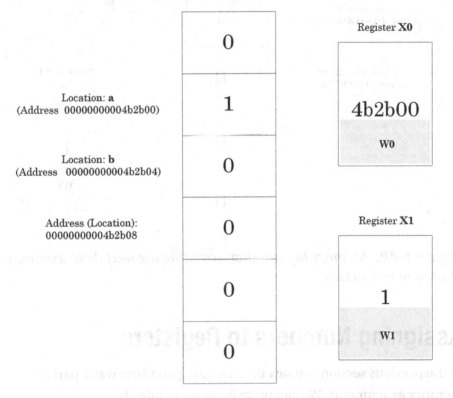

Figure 1-4A. *Memory layout after executing the first three assembly language instructions*

After executing the next three assembly language instructions, we have the memory layout shown in Figure 1-4B.

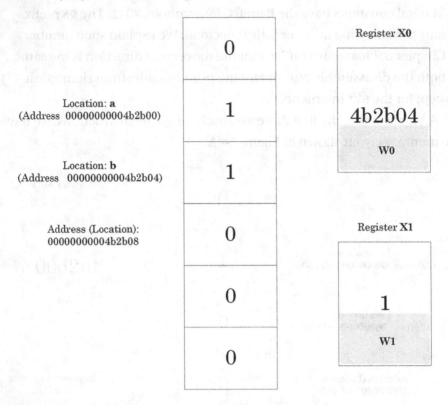

Figure 1-4B. *Memory layout after executing the next three assembly language instructions*

Assigning Numbers to Registers

In the previous section, we saw that assigning numbers was a part of memory assignments. We can write in pseudo-code:

```
register <- 1
register <- [a]
```

Note that we do not use brackets when we refer to register contents. The latter instruction means assigning (copying) the number at the location (address) "a" to a register.

In assembly language, we write

```
mov  w1, #1          // 1 is copied to the first half of X1
                        register
mov  x1, #1          // full contents of X1 register are
                        replaced with 1
adr  x0, a           // copy the location (address) "a" to
                        X0 register
ldr  w1, [x0]        // copy the number at the location
                        stored in X0 to
                     // the first half of X1 register
Ldr  x1, [x0]        // copy the number at the location
                        stored in X0 to X1
```

In the GDB disassembly output, we may see the output where one adr instruction is replaced by adrp/add instructions with parts of the address value:

```
adrp x0, 0x4b2000    // 0x4b2000 + 0xb00 = 0x4b2b00
                        ("a" address)
add  x0, x0, #0xb00
ldr  w1, [x0]
```

"Arithmetic" Project: Adding Numbers to Memory Cells

Now let's look at the following pseudo-code statement in more detail:

```
[b] <- [b] + [a]
```

To recall, "a" and "b" mean the names of locations (addresses) 00000000004b2b00 and 00000000004b2b04, respectively (see Figures 1-4A and 1-4B). [a] and [b] mean contents at addresses "a" and "b," respectively, simply some numbers stored there.

In the C or C++ language, we write the following statement:

```
b = b + a;
b += a;
```

In assembly language, we use the instruction ADD. Because of ARM architecture limitations, we cannot use memory addresses in one step (instruction), for example, **add b, b, a**. We can only use the **add register1, register1, register0** instruction to add the value stored in the **register0** to the value stored in the **register1** and move the result to the **register1**. So, first, we need to load (ldr) contents at addresses "a" and "b" to registers and store (str) the result back to the memory location "b" after addition. Recall that a register is like a temporary memory cell itself here:

```
Register2 <- [b]
Register1 <- [a]
Register2 <- register2 + register1
[b] <- register2
```

In assembly language, we write

```
adr  x0, b
ldr  w1, [x0]
adr  x0, a
ldr  w0, [x0]
add  w1, w1, w0
adr  x0, b
str  w1, [x0]
```

In the GDB disassembly output, we may see the following code:

```
adrp x0, 0x4b2000
add  x0, x0, #0xb00
ldr  w1, [x0]
adrp x0, 0x4b2000
add  x0, x0, #0xb04
ldr  w0, [x0]
add  w1, w1, w0
adrp x0, 0x4b2000
add  x0, x0, #0xb04
str  w1, [x0]
```

Now we can translate our pseudo-code into assembly language:

[a] <- 1	// x0 = a	adr x0, a
	// w1 = 1	mov w1, #1
	// [a] = 1	str w1, [x0]
[b] <- 1	// x0 = b	adr x0, b
	// w1 = 1	mov w1, #1
	// [b] = 1	str w1, [x0]
[b] <- [b] + [a]	**// x0 = b**	**adr x0, b**
	// w1 = 1	**ldr w1, [x0]**
	// x0 = a	**adr x0, a**
	// w0 = 1	**ldr w0, [x0]**
	// w1 = 2	**add w1, w1, w0**
	// x0 = b	**adr x0, b**
	// [b] = 2	**str w1, [x0]**
[a] <- [a] + 1		
[b] <- [b] * [a]		

After executing ADR, LDR, ADD, and STR instructions, we have the memory layout illustrated in Figure 1-5.

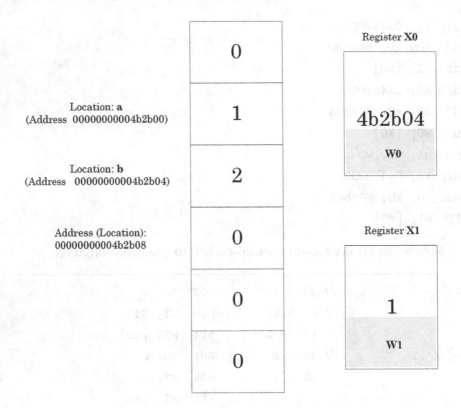

Figure 1-5. *Memory layout after executing ADR, LDR, ADD, and STR instructions*

Incrementing/Decrementing Numbers in Memory and Registers

In pseudo-code, it looks simple and means increment (decrement) a number stored at the location (address) "a":

```
[a] <- [a] + 1
[a] <- [a] - 1
```

In the C or C++ language, we can write this using three possible ways:

```
a = a + 1;
++a;
a++;
b = b - 1;
--b;
b--;
```

In assembly language, we use instructions ADD and SUB and write

```
add   x0, x0, #1
sub   x0, x0, #1

adr   x0, a
ldr   w1, [x0]
add   w1, w1, #1
str   w1, [x0]

adr   x0, b
ldr   w1, [x0]
sub   w1, w1, #1
str   w1, [x0]
```

In the GDB disassembly output, we may see the similar instructions:

```
adrp x0, 0x4b2000
add   x0, x0, #0xb00
ldr   w0, [x0]
add   w1, w0, #0x1
adrp x0, 0x4b2000
add   x0, x0, #0xb00
str   w1, [x0]
```

Now we add the assembly language translation of increment:

```
[a] <- 1            // x0 = a          adr  x0, a
                    // w1 = 1          mov  w1, #1
                    // [a] = 1         str  w1, [x0]
[b] <- 1            // x0 = b          adr  x0, b
                    // w1 = 1          mov  w1, #1
                    // [b] = 1         str  w1, [x0]
[b] <- [b] + [a]   // x0 = b          adr  x0, b
                    // w1 = 1          ldr  w1, [x0]
                    // x0 = a          adr  x0, a
                    // w0 = 1          ldr  w0, [x0]
                    // w1 = 2          add  w1, w1, w0
                    // x0 = b          adr  x0, b
                    // [b] = 2         str  w1, [x0]
[a] <- [a] + 1     // x0 = a          adr  x0, a
                    // w1 = 1          ldr  w1, [x0]
                    // w1 = 2          add  w1, w1, #1
                    // [a] = 2         str  w1, [x0]
[b] <- [b] * [a]
```

After the execution of the ADD instruction, we have the memory layout illustrated in Figure 1-6.

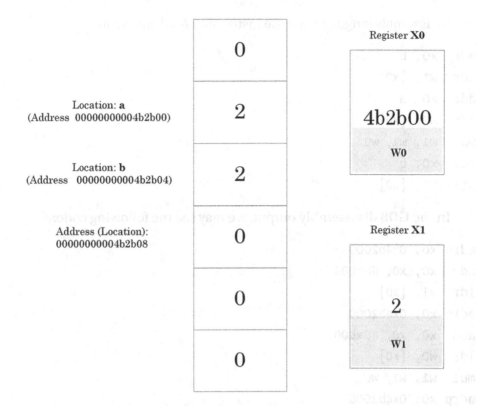

Figure 1-6. *Memory layout after the execution of the ADD instruction*

Multiplying Numbers

In pseudo-code, we write

[b] <- [b] * [a]

It means that we multiply the number at the location (address) "b" by the number at the location (address) "a."

In the C or C++ language, we can write that using two ways:

```
b = b * a;
b *= a;
```

In assembly language, we use instruction MUL and write

```
adr  x0, b
ldr  w1, [x0]
adr  x0, a
ldr  w0, [x0]
mul  w1, w1, w0
adr  x0, b
str  w1, [x0]
```

In the GDB disassembly output, we may see the following code:

```
adrp x0, 0x4b2000
add  x0, x0, #0xb04
ldr  w1, [x0]
adrp x0, 0x4b2000
add  x0, x0, #0xb00
ldr  w0, [x0]
mul  w1, w1, w0
adrp x0, 0x4b2000
add  x0, x0, #0xb04
str  w1, [x0]
```

Now we add additional assembly instructions to our pseudo-code assembly language translation:

[a] <- 1	// x0 = a	adr x0, a
	// w1 = 1	mov w1, #1
	// [a] = 1	str w1, [x0]
[b] <- 1	// x0 = b	adr x0, b
	// w1 = 1	mov w1, #1
	// [b] = 1	str w1, [x0]
[b] <- [b] + [a]	// x0 = b	adr x0, b
	// w1 = 1	ldr w1, [x0]
	// x0 = a	adr x0, a
	// w0 = 1	ldr w0, [x0]
	// w1 = 2	add w1, w1, w0
	// x0 = b	adr x0, b
	// [b] = 2	str w1, [x0]
[a] <- [a] + 1	// x0 = a	adr x0, a
	// w1 = 1	ldr w1, [x0]
	// w1 = 2	add w1, w1, #1
	// [a] = 2	str w1, [x0]
[b] <- [b] * [a]	**// x0 = b**	**adr x0, b**
	// w1 = 2	**ldr w1, [x0]**
	// x0 = a	**adr x0, a**
	// w0 = 2	**ldr w0, [x0]**
	// w1 = 4	**mul w1, w1, w0**
	// x0 = b	**adr x0, b**
	// [b] = 4	**str w1, [x0]**

After the execution of the STR instruction, we have the memory layout illustrated in Figure 1-7.

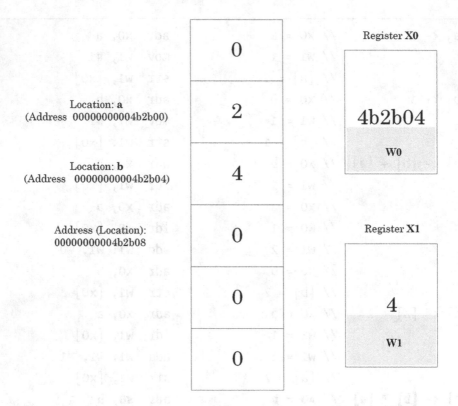

Figure 1-7. *Memory layout after the execution of the STR instruction*

Summary

This chapter introduced CPU registers and explained the memory layout of a simple arithmetic program. We learned basic ARM64 commands, including loading values from and storing values in memory. We also manually translated C and C++ code to assembly language.

The next chapter looks at assembly language code produced by a debugger via disassembling binary code. Then, we reverse it to C and C++ code. We also compare the disassembly output of nonoptimized code to optimized code.

CHAPTER 2

Code Optimization

"Arithmetic" Project: C/C++ Program

Let's rewrite our "Arithmetic" program in C/C++. Corresponding assembly language instructions are put in comments:

```c
int a, b;

int main(int argc, char* argv[])
{
    a = 1;              // adr  x0, a
                        // mov  w1, #1
                        // str  w1, [x0]

    b = 1;              // adr  x0, b
                        // mov  w1, #1
                        // str  w1, [x0]

    b = b + a;          // adr  x0, b
                        // ldr  w1, [x0]
                        // adr  x0, a
                        // ldr  w0, [x0]
                        // add  w1, w1, w0
                        // adr  x0, b
                        // str  w1, [x0]
```

© Dmitry Vostokov 2023
D. Vostokov, *Foundations of ARM64 Linux Debugging, Disassembling, and Reversing*,
https://doi.org/10.1007/978-1-4842-9082-8_2

```
    ++a;                    // adr   x0, a
                            // ldr   w1, [x0]
                            // add   w1, w1, #1
                            // str   w1, [x0]

    b = b * a;              // adr   x0, b
                            // ldr   w1, [x0]
                            // adr   x0, a
                            // ldr   w0, [x0]
                            // mul   w1, w1, w0
                            // adr   x0, b
                            // str   w1, [x0]

                            // results: [a] = 2 and [b] = 4
    return 0;
}
```

Downloading GDB

We used one of the free ARM64 Linux compute instances available from cloud providers. In our case, GDB was already available after provisioning. If, in your case, GDB is not available, you need to install it together with basic build tools. For example, in Debian:

```
$ sudo apt install build-essential
$ sudo apt install gdb
```

You may also need to download git to clone source code:

```
$ sudo apt install git
$ cd ~
$ git clone github.com/apress/arm64-linux-debugging-
disassembling-reversing .
```

On our RHEL-type system, we updated the tools (git included) and GDB via

```
$ sudo yum group install "Development Tools"
$ sudo yum install gdb
```

GDB Disassembly Output – No Optimization

The source code can be downloaded from the following location:

github.com/apress/arm64-linux-debugging-disassembling-reversing/Chapter2/

If we compile and link the program in no optimization mode (default):

```
$ gcc ArithmeticProjectC.cpp -o ArithmeticProjectC
```

we get the binary executable module we can load in GDB and inspect assembly code.

First, we run GDB with the program as a parameter:

```
$ gdb ./ArithmeticProjectC
GNU gdb (GDB) Red Hat Enterprise Linux 7.6.1-120.0.2.el7
Copyright (C) 2013 Free Software Foundation, Inc.
License GPLv3+: GNU GPL version 3 or later <http://gnu.org/
licenses/gpl.html>
This is free software: you are free to change and
redistribute it.
There is NO WARRANTY, to the extent permitted by law.  Type
"show copying"
and "show warranty" for details.
This GDB was configured as "aarch64-redhat-linux-gnu".
For bug reporting instructions, please see:
<http://www.gnu.org/software/gdb/bugs/>...
```

Reading symbols from /home/coredump/pflddr/A64/Chapter2/
ArithmeticProjectC...(no debugging symbols found)...done.
(gdb)

Next, we put a breakpoint at our *main* C/C++ function to allow the
program execution to stop at that point and give us a chance to inspect
memory and registers. Symbolic names/function names like "main" can be
used instead of code memory locations:

```
(gdb) break main
Breakpoint 1 at 0x4005bc
```

Then we start the execution of the program (let it **run**). The program
then stops at the previously set breakpoint:

```
Starting program: /home/coredump/pflddr/A64/Chapter2/./
ArithmeticProjectC

Breakpoint 1, 0x00000000004005bc in main ()
Missing separate debuginfos, use: debuginfo-install
glibc-2.17-325.0.2.el7_9.aarch64
```

Now we **disass**emble the *main* function:

```
(gdb) disass main
Dump of assembler code for function main:
   0x00000000004005b8 <+0>:     sub     sp, sp, #0x10
=> 0x00000000004005bc <+4>:     str     w0, [sp,#12]
   0x00000000004005c0 <+8>:     str     x1, [sp]
   0x00000000004005c4 <+12>:    adrp    x0, 0x420000
   0x00000000004005c8 <+16>:    add     x0, x0, #0x20
   0x00000000004005cc <+20>:    mov     w1, #0x1              // #1
   0x00000000004005d0 <+24>:    str     w1, [x0]
   0x00000000004005d4 <+28>:    adrp    x0, 0x420000
   0x00000000004005d8 <+32>:    add     x0, x0, #0x24
```

```
0x00000000004005dc <+36>:       mov     w1, #0x1              // #1
0x00000000004005e0 <+40>:       str     w1, [x0]
0x00000000004005e4 <+44>:       adrp    x0, 0x420000
0x00000000004005e8 <+48>:       add     x0, x0, #0x24
0x00000000004005ec <+52>:       ldr     w1, [x0]
0x00000000004005f0 <+56>:       adrp    x0, 0x420000
0x00000000004005f4 <+60>:       add     x0, x0, #0x20
0x00000000004005f8 <+64>:       ldr     w0, [x0]
0x00000000004005fc <+68>:       add     w1, w1, w0
0x0000000000400600 <+72>:       adrp    x0, 0x420000
0x0000000000400604 <+76>:       add     x0, x0, #0x24
0x0000000000400608 <+80>:       str     w1, [x0]
0x000000000040060c <+84>:       adrp    x0, 0x420000
0x0000000000400610 <+88>:       add     x0, x0, #0x20
0x0000000000400614 <+92>:       ldr     w0, [x0]
0x0000000000400618 <+96>:       add     w1, w0, #0x1
0x000000000040061c <+100>:      adrp    x0, 0x420000
0x0000000000400620 <+104>:      add     x0, x0, #0x20
0x0000000000400624 <+108>:      str     w1, [x0]
---Type <return> to continue, or q <return> to quit---
0x0000000000400628 <+112>:      adrp    x0, 0x420000
0x000000000040062c <+116>:      add     x0, x0, #0x24
0x0000000000400630 <+120>:      ldr     w1, [x0]
0x0000000000400634 <+124>:      adrp    x0, 0x420000
0x0000000000400638 <+128>:      add     x0, x0, #0x20
0x000000000040063c <+132>:      ldr     w0, [x0]
0x0000000000400640 <+136>:      mul     w1, w1, w0
0x0000000000400644 <+140>:      adrp    x0, 0x420000
0x0000000000400648 <+144>:      add     x0, x0, #0x24
0x000000000040064c <+148>:      str     w1, [x0]
```

```
0x0000000000400650 <+152>:    mov    w0, #0x0                // #0
0x0000000000400654 <+156>:    add    sp, sp, #0x10
0x0000000000400658 <+160>:    ret
End of assembler dump.
```

We repeat the part of the formatted disassembly output here that corresponds to our C/C++ code:

```
0x00000000004005c4 <+12>:     adrp   x0, 0x420000
0x00000000004005c8 <+16>:     add    x0, x0, #0x20
0x00000000004005cc <+20>:     mov    w1, #0x1
0x00000000004005d0 <+24>:     str    w1, [x0]
0x00000000004005d4 <+28>:     adrp   x0, 0x420000
0x00000000004005d8 <+32>:     add    x0, x0, #0x24
0x00000000004005dc <+36>:     mov    w1, #0x1
0x00000000004005e0 <+40>:     str    w1, [x0]
0x00000000004005e4 <+44>:     adrp   x0, 0x420000
0x00000000004005e8 <+48>:     add    x0, x0, #0x24
0x00000000004005ec <+52>:     ldr    w1, [x0]
0x00000000004005f0 <+56>:     adrp   x0, 0x420000
0x00000000004005f4 <+60>:     add    x0, x0, #0x20
0x00000000004005f8 <+64>:     ldr    w0, [x0]
0x00000000004005fc <+68>:     add    w1, w1, w0
0x0000000000400600 <+72>:     adrp   x0, 0x420000
0x0000000000400604 <+76>:     add    x0, x0, #0x24
0x0000000000400608 <+80>:     str    w1, [x0]
0x000000000040060c <+84>:     adrp   x0, 0x420000
0x0000000000400610 <+88>:     add    x0, x0, #0x20
0x0000000000400614 <+92>:     ldr    w0, [x0]
0x0000000000400618 <+96>:     add    w1, w0, #0x1
0x000000000040061c <+100>:    adrp   x0, 0x420000
0x0000000000400620 <+104>:    add    x0, x0, #0x20
```

```
0x0000000000400624 <+108>:    str     w1, [x0]
0x0000000000400628 <+112>:    adrp    x0, 0x420000
0x000000000040062c <+116>:    add     x0, x0, #0x24
0x0000000000400630 <+120>:    ldr     w1, [x0]
0x0000000000400634 <+124>:    adrp    x0, 0x420000
0x0000000000400638 <+128>:    add     x0, x0, #0x20
0x000000000040063c <+132>:    ldr     w0, [x0]
0x0000000000400640 <+136>:    mul     w1, w1, w0
0x0000000000400644 <+140>:    adrp    x0, 0x420000
0x0000000000400648 <+144>:    add     x0, x0, #0x24
0x000000000040064c <+148>:    str     w1, [x0]
```

We can directly translate it to bare assembly code we used in the previous chapter and put corresponding pseudo-code in comments (memory addresses may be different on your system):

```
    0x00000000004005c4 <+12>:     adrp    x0, 0x420000
// [a] <- 1
    0x00000000004005c8 <+16>:     add     x0, x0, #0x20
    0x00000000004005cc <+20>:     mov     w1, #0x1
    0x00000000004005d0 <+24>:     str     w1, [x0]
    0x00000000004005d4 <+28>:     adrp    x0, 0x420000
// [b] <- 1
    0x00000000004005d8 <+32>:     add     x0, x0, #0x24
    0x00000000004005dc <+36>:     mov     w1, #0x1
    0x00000000004005e0 <+40>:     str     w1, [x0]
    0x00000000004005e4 <+44>:     adrp    x0, 0x420000
// [b] <- [b] + [a]
    0x00000000004005e8 <+48>:     add     x0, x0, #0x24
    0x00000000004005ec <+52>:     ldr     w1, [x0]
    0x00000000004005f0 <+56>:     adrp    x0, 0x420000
    0x00000000004005f4 <+60>:     add     x0, x0, #0x20
```

```
    0x00000000004005f8 <+64>:       ldr     w0, [x0]
    0x00000000004005fc <+68>:       add     w1, w1, w0
    0x0000000000400600 <+72>:       adrp    x0, 0x420000
    0x0000000000400604 <+76>:       add     x0, x0, #0x24
    0x0000000000400608 <+80>:       str     w1, [x0]
    0x000000000040060c <+84>:       adrp    x0, 0x420000
// [a] <- [a] + 1
    0x0000000000400610 <+88>:       add     x0, x0, #0x20
    0x0000000000400614 <+92>:       ldr     w0, [x0]
    0x0000000000400618 <+96>:       add     w1, w0, #0x1
    0x000000000040061c <+100>:      adrp    x0, 0x420000
    0x0000000000400620 <+104>:      add     x0, x0, #0x20
    0x0000000000400624 <+108>:      str     w1, [x0]
    0x0000000000400628 <+112>:      adrp    x0, 0x420000
// [b] <- [b] * [a]
    0x000000000040062c <+116>:      add     x0, x0, #0x24
    0x0000000000400630 <+120>:      ldr     w1, [x0]
    0x0000000000400634 <+124>:      adrp    x0, 0x420000
    0x0000000000400638 <+128>:      add     x0, x0, #0x20
    0x000000000040063c <+132>:      ldr     w0, [x0]
    0x0000000000400640 <+136>:      mul     w1, w1, w0
    0x0000000000400644 <+140>:      adrp    x0, 0x420000
    0x0000000000400648 <+144>:      add     x0, x0, #0x24
    0x000000000040064c <+148>:      str     w1, [x0]
```

Now we can exit GDB:

```
(gdb) q
A debugging session is active.

        Inferior 1 [process 11103] will be killed.

Quit anyway? (y or n) y
$
```

GDB Disassembly Output – Optimization

If we compile and link the program in optimization mode:

```
$ gcc ArithmeticProjectC.cpp -O1 -o ArithmeticProjectC
```

and after repeating the same steps in GDB, we get the following output:

```
(gdb) disass main
Dump of assembler code for function main:
   0x00000000004005b8 <+0>:      adrp    x0, 0x420000
   0x00000000004005bc <+4>:      add     x1, x0, #0x20
   0x00000000004005c0 <+8>:      mov     w2, #0x2        // #2
=> 0x00000000004005c4 <+12>:     str     w2, [x0,#32]
   0x00000000004005c8 <+16>:     mov     w0, #0x4        // #4
   0x00000000004005cc <+20>:     str     w0, [x1,#4]
   0x00000000004005d0 <+24>:     mov     w0, #0x0        // #0
   0x00000000004005d4 <+28>:     ret
```

This corresponds to the following pseudo-code:

```
[a] <- 2
[b] <- 4
```

The calculation of memory addresses is a bit more complex:

```
   0x00000000004005b8 <+0>:   adrp  x0, 0x420000
   0x00000000004005bc <+4>:   add   x1, x0, #0x20      // x1 = x0 +
                                                       // 0x20 = a
   0x00000000004005c0 <+8>:   mov   w2, #0x2           // w2 = 2
=> 0x00000000004005c4 <+12>:  str   w2, [x0,#32]       // #32 in 0x20
                                                       // [a] = [x0
                                                       // + 0x20] = 2
   0x00000000004005c8 <+16>:  mov   w0, #0x4           // w0 = 4
   0x00000000004005cc <+20>:  str   w0, [x1,#4]        // [b] = [a
                                                       // + 4] = 4
```

27

What happened to all our assembly code in this executable? This code seems to be directly placing the end result into "a" and "b" memory cells if we observe. Why is this happening? The answer lies in compiler optimization. When the code is compiled in optimization mode, the compiler can calculate the final result from the simple C/C++ source code itself and generate only the necessary code to update corresponding memory locations.

Summary

In this chapter, we looked at assembly language code produced by a debugger via disassembling binary code. Then, we reversed it to C and C++ code. We also compared the disassembly output of nonoptimized code to optimized code and understood why.

The next chapter refreshes number representations, especially the hexadecimal one.

CHAPTER 3

Number Representations

Numbers and Their Representations

Imagine a herder in ancient times trying to count his sheep. He has a certain number of stones (twelve):

However, he can only count up to three and arranges the total into groups of three:

D. Vostokov, *Foundations of ARM64 Linux Debugging, Disassembling, and Reversing*,
https://doi.org/10.1007/978-1-4842-9082-8_3

The last picture is a representation (a kind of notation) of the number of stones. We have one group of three groups of three stones plus a separate group of three stones. If he could count up to ten, we would see a different representation of the same number of stones. We would have one group of ten stones and another group of two stones.

Decimal Representation (Base Ten)

Let's now see how twelve stones are represented in arithmetic notation if we can count up to ten. We have one group of ten numbers plus two:

$$12_{dec} = 1 * 10 + 2 \text{ or } 1 * 10^1 + 2 * 10^0$$

Here is another exercise with 123 stones. We have **1** group of ten by ten stones, another group of **2** groups of ten stones, and the last group of **3** stones:

$$\mathbf{123}_{dec} = \mathbf{1} * 10*10 + \mathbf{2} * 10 + \mathbf{3} \text{ or } \mathbf{1} * 10^2 + \mathbf{2} * 10^1 + \mathbf{3} * 10^0$$

We can formalize it in the following summation notation:

$$N_{dec} = a_n*10^n + a_{n-1}*10^{n-1} + ... + a_2*10^2 + a_1*10^1 + a_0*10^0$$
$$0 <= a_i <= 9$$

Using the summation symbol, we have this formula:

$$N_{dec} = \sum_{i=0}^{n} a_i*10^i$$

Ternary Representation (Base Three)

Now we come back to our herder's example of twelve stones. We have **1** group of three by three stones, **1** group of three stones, and an empty (**0**) group (which is not empty if we have one stone only or have thirteen stones instead of twelve). We can write down the number of groups sequentially: **110**. Therefore, 110 is a ternary representation (notation) of twelve stones, and it is equivalent to 12 written in decimal notation:

$$12_{dec} = 1*3^2 + 1*3^1 + 0*3^0$$

$$N_{dec} = a_n*3^n + a_{n-1}*3^{n-1} + ... + a_2*3^2 + a_1*3^1 + a_0*3^0$$
$$a_i = 0 \text{ or } 1 \text{ or } 2$$

$$N_{dec} = \sum_{i=0}^{n} a_i*3^i$$

Binary Representation (Base Two)

In the case of counting up to two, we have more groups for twelve stones: **1100**. Therefore, 1100 is a binary representation (notation) for 12 in decimal notation:

$$12_{dec} = 1*2^3 + 1*2^2 + 0*2^1 + 0*2^0$$

$$123_{dec} = 1*2^6 + 1*2^5 + 1*2^4 + 1*2^3 + 0*2^2 + 1*2^1 + 1*2^0 \text{ or }$$
$$1111011_2$$

$$N_{dec} = a_n*2^n + a_{n-1}*2^{n-1} + ... + a_2*2^2 + a_1*2^1 + a_0*2^0$$
$$a_i = 0 \text{ or } 1$$

$$N_{dec} = \sum_{i=0}^{n} a_i*2^i$$

Hexadecimal Representation (Base Sixteen)

If we can count up to sixteen, twelve stones fit in one group, but we need more symbols: A, B, C, D, E, and F for ten, eleven, twelve, thirteen, fourteen, and fifteen, respectively:

12_{dec} = C in hexadecimal representation (notation)

$123_{dec} = 7B_{hex}$

$123_{dec} = 7*16^1 + 11*16^0$

$$N_{dec} = \sum_{i=0}^{n} a_i*16^i$$

Why Are Hexadecimals Used?

Consider this number written in binary notation: 110001010011_2. Its equivalent in decimal notation is 3155:

$$3155_{dec} = 1*2^{11} + 1*2^{10} + 0*2^9 + 0*2^8 + 0*2^7 + 1*2^6 + 0*2^5$$
$$+ 1*2^4 + 0*2^3 + 0*2^2 + 1*2^1 + 1*2^0$$

Now we divide the binary number digits into groups of four and write them down in decimal and hexadecimal notation:

1100_0101_0011

12$_{dec}$ **5**$_{dec}$ **3**$_{dec}$

C$_{hex}$ **5**$_{hex}$ **3**$_{hex}$

We see that hexadecimal notation is more compact because every four binary digit group number corresponds to one hexadecimal number. Table 3-1 lists hexadecimal equivalents for every four binary digit combination.

Table 3-1. *Hexadecimal Equivalents for Every Four Binary Digit Combination*

Binary	Decimal	Hexadecimal
0000	0	0
0001	1	1
0010	2	2
0011	3	3
0100	4	4
0101	5	5
0110	6	6
0111	7	7
1000	8	8
1001	9	9
1010	10	A
1011	11	B
1100	12	C
1101	13	D
1110	14	E
1111	15	F

In GDB and other debuggers, memory addresses are displayed in hexadecimal notation.

Summary

This chapter refreshed different representations of a number, including hexadecimal notation.

The next chapter introduces pointers. We rewrite our arithmetic program from Chapter 1 using pointers to memory and use the GDB debugger to execute instructions one by one and watch changes to memory.

CHAPTER 4

Pointers

A Definition

The concept of a pointer is one of the most important to understand thoroughly to master Linux debugging. By definition, a pointer is a memory cell or a processor register that contains the address of another memory cell, as shown in Figure 4-1. It has its own address as any memory cell. Sometimes, a pointer is called an indirect address (vs. a direct address, the address of a memory cell). Iteratively, we can define another level of indirection and introduce a pointer to a pointer as a memory cell or a processor register that contains the address of another memory cell that contains the address of another memory cell, and so on.

© Dmitry Vostokov 2023
D. Vostokov, *Foundations of ARM64 Linux Debugging, Disassembling, and Reversing*,
https://doi.org/10.1007/978-1-4842-9082-8_4

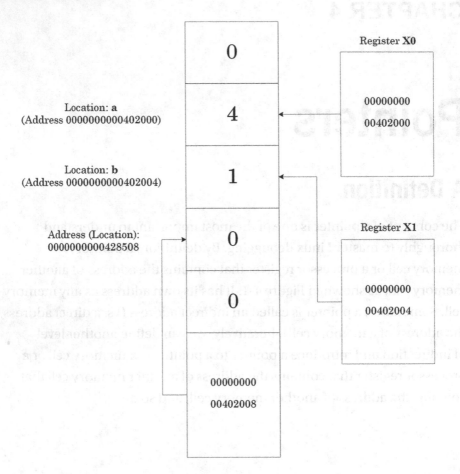

Figure 4-1. *Example pointers and memory layout*

"Pointers" Project: Memory Layout and Registers

In our debugging project, we have two memory addresses (locations), "a" and "b." We can think about "a" and "b" as names of addresses (locations). We remind that notation (a) means contents at the memory address (location) "a."

We also have registers X0 and X1 as pointers to "a" and "b." These registers contain addresses of "a" and "b," respectively. The notation [X0] means the contents of a memory cell whose address is in the register X0.

In C and C++ languages, we declare and define pointers to "a" and "b" as

```
int *a, *b;
```

Our project memory layout before program execution is shown in Figure 4-2. Addresses always occupy 64-bit memory cells or full 64-bit registers like X0 or X1 (they cannot fit in W0 or W1 or a 32-bit memory cell). We also use lower halves of X2–X4 registers (W2-W4) to hold temporary integer values if necessary.

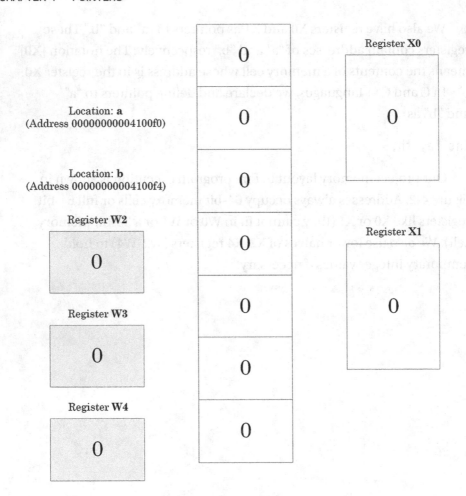

Figure 4-2. *Project memory layout before program execution*

"Pointers" Project: Calculations

In order to understand pointers better from a low-level assembly language perspective, we perform our old arithmetic calculations from Chapter 1 using pointers to memory instead of direct memory addresses:

```
X0 <- address a
[X0] <- 1
X1 <- address b
[X1] <- 1
[X1] <- [X1] + [X0]
[X0] <- [X0] + 1
[X1] <- [X1] * [X0]
```

Using Pointers to Assign Numbers to Memory Cells

First, the following sequence of pseudo-code instructions means that we interpret the contents of the X0 register as the address of a memory cell and then assign a value to that memory cell:

```
X0 <- address a
[X0] <- 1
```

In C and C++ languages, it is called "dereferencing a pointer," and we write

```
int a;
int *pa = &a; // declaration and definition of a pointer
*pa = 1;       // get a memory cell (dereference a pointer)
               // and assign a value to it
```

In assembly language, we write

```
adr  x0, a    // load the address "a" into x0
mov  w3, #1   // set the temporary register to 1
str  w3, [x0] // use x0 as a pointer and store 1 at the memory
              // address in x0
```

In the GDB disassembly output, we see something like this:

```
0x00000000004000b0 <+0>:      adr    x0, 0x4100f0
0x00000000004000b4 <+4>:      mov    w3, #0x1
0x00000000004000b8 <+8>:      str    w3, [x0]
```

The source code for this chapter can be downloaded from

github.com/apress/arm64-linux-debugging-disassembling-reversing/Chapter4/

To illustrate some instructions and not to be dependent on how the compiler translates C/C++ code, we wrote the program in assembly language. We need to compile and link it first before loading it into GDB and then disassemble its *main* function as described in Chapter 2.

```
$ as PointersProject.asm -o PointersProject.o

$ ld PointersProject.o -o PointersProject

$ gdb ./PointersProject
GNU gdb (GDB) Red Hat Enterprise Linux 7.6.1-120.0.2.el7
Copyright (C) 2013 Free Software Foundation, Inc.
License GPLv3+: GNU GPL version 3 or later <http://gnu.org/
licenses/gpl.html>
This is free software: you are free to change and
redistribute it.
There is NO WARRANTY, to the extent permitted by law.  Type
"show copying"
and "show warranty" for details.
This GDB was configured as "aarch64-redhat-linux-gnu".
For bug reporting instructions, please see:
<http://www.gnu.org/software/gdb/bugs/>...
```

Reading symbols from /home/coredump/pflddr/A64/Chapter4/
PointersProject...(no debugging symbols found)...done.
(gdb)

We put a breakpoint on the *main* function, run the program until GDB
breaks in, and then disassemble the *main* function:

```
(gdb) break main
Breakpoint 1 at 0x4000b0
```

```
(gdb) run
Starting program: /home/coredump/pflddr/A64/Chapter4/./
PointersProject
```

```
Breakpoint 1, 0x0000000000401000 in _start ()
```

```
(gdb) disass main
Dump of assembler code for function _start:
=> 0x00000000004000b0 <+0>:     adr     x0, 0x4100f0
   0x00000000004000b4 <+4>:     mov     w3, #0x1          // #1
   0x00000000004000b8 <+8>:     str     w3, [x0]
   0x00000000004000bc <+12>:    adr     x1, 0x4100f4
   0x00000000004000c0 <+16>:    str     w3, [x1]
   0x00000000004000c4 <+20>:    ldr     w2, [x0]
   0x00000000004000c8 <+24>:    ldr     w3, [x1]
   0x00000000004000cc <+28>:    add     w4, w3, w2
   0x00000000004000d0 <+32>:    str     w4, [x1]
   0x00000000004000d4 <+36>:    add     w2, w2, #0x1
   0x00000000004000d8 <+40>:    str     w2, [x0]
   0x00000000004000dc <+44>:    mul     w3, w4, w2
   0x00000000004000e0 <+48>:    str     w3, [x1]
   0x00000000004000e4 <+52>:    mov     x0, #0x0          // #0
   0x00000000004000e8 <+56>:    mov     w8, #0x5d         // #93
   0x00000000004000ec <+60>:    svc     #0x0
End of assembler dump.
```

Now we examine variables "a" and "b" to verify the memory layout shown previously in Figure 4-2 using the **info variables** GDB command:

```
(gdb) info variables
All defined variables:

Non-debugging symbols:
0x00000000004100f0  a
0x00000000004100f4  b
0x00000000004100f8  __bss_end__
0x00000000004100f8  __bss_start
0x00000000004100f8  __bss_start__
0x00000000004100f8  __end__
0x00000000004100f8  _bss_end__
0x00000000004100f8  _edata
0x00000000004100f8  _end
```

We also verify that the values of X0 and X1 registers are in accordance with Figure 4-2:

```
(gdb) info registers x0 x1
x0              0x0         0
x1              0x0         0
```

We instruct GDB to automatically display the current instruction to be executed; the values of registers X0, X1, W2, W3, and W4; and the contents of variables "a" and "b":

```
(gdb) display/i $pc
1: x/i $pc
=> 0x4000b0 <main>:     adr     x0, 0x4100f0

(gdb) display/x $x0
2: /x $x0 = 0x0
```

```
(gdb) display/x $x1
3: /x $x1 = 0x0

(gdb) display/x $w2
4: /x $w2 = 0x0

(gdb) display/x $w3
5: /x $w3 = 0x0
(gdb) display/x $w4
6: /x $w4 = 0x0

(gdb) display/x (int)a
7: /x (int)a = 0x0

(gdb) display/x (int)b
8: /x (int)b = 0x0
```

Now we execute the first five instructions that correspond to our pseudo-code using the **stepi** GDB command or **si** (shorter command version):

X0 <- address a		**adr x0, 0x4100f0**
		mov w3, #0x1
[X0] <- 1	**// [a] = 1**	**str w3, [x0]**
X1 <- address b		**adr x1, 0x4100f4**
[X1] <- 1	**// [b] = 1**	**str w3, [x1]**
[X1] <- [X1] + [X0]		
[X0] <- [X0] + 1		
[X1] <- [X1] * [X0]		

```
(gdb) si
0x00000000004000b4 in main ()
8: /x (int)b = 0x0
7: /x (int)a = 0x0
6: /x $w4 = 0x0
```

```
5: /x $w3 = 0x0
4: /x $w2 = 0x0
3: /x $x1 = 0x0
2: /x $x0 = 0x4100f0
1: x/i $pc
=> 0x4000b4 <main+4>:   mov     w3, #0x1            // #1

(gdb) si
0x00000000004000b8 in main ()
8: /x (int)b = 0x0
7: /x (int)a = 0x0
6: /x $w4 = 0x0
5: /x $w3 = 0x1
4: /x $w2 = 0x0
3: /x $x1 = 0x0
2: /x $x0 = 0x4100f0
1: x/i $pc
=> 0x4000b8 <main+8>:   str     w3, [x0]

(gdb) si
0x00000000004000bc in main ()
8: /x (int)b = 0x0
7: /x (int)a = 0x1
6: /x $w4 = 0x0
5: /x $w3 = 0x1
4: /x $w2 = 0x0
3: /x $x1 = 0x0
2: /x $x0 = 0x4100f0
1: x/i $pc
=> 0x4000bc <main+12>:  adr     x1, 0x4100f4
```

```
(gdb) si
0x00000000004000c0 in main ()
8: /x (int)b = 0x0
7: /x (int)a = 0x1
6: /x $w4 = 0x0
5: /x $w3 = 0x1
4: /x $w2 = 0x0
3: /x $x1 = 0x4100f4
2: /x $x0 = 0x4100f0
1: x/i $pc
=> 0x4000c0 <main+16>:   str     w3, [x1]

(gdb) si
0x00000000004000c4 in main ()
8: /x (int)b = 0x1
7: /x (int)a = 0x1
6: /x $w4 = 0x0
5: /x $w3 = 0x1
4: /x $w2 = 0x0
3: /x $x1 = 0x4100f4
2: /x $x0 = 0x4100f0
1: x/i $pc
=> 0x4000c4 <main+20>:   ldr     w2, [x0]
```

All this corresponds to a memory layout shown in Figure 4-3.

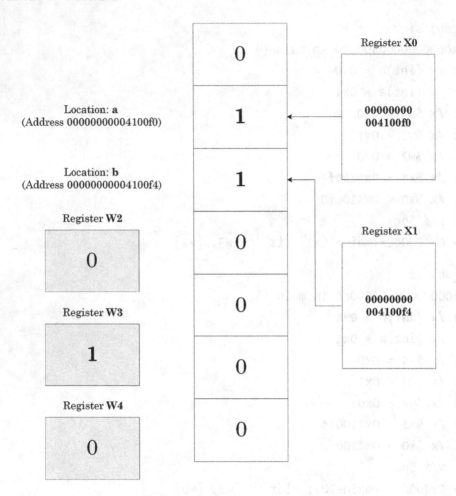

Figure 4-3. *Memory layout after executing the first five instructions*

Adding Numbers Using Pointers

Now we look at the next pseudo-code statement:

```
[X1] <- [X1] + [X0]
```

Recall that [X0] and [X1] mean contents of memory cells whose addresses (locations) are stored in X0 and X1 CPU registers. The preceding statement is equivalent to the following C or C++ language expression where the "*" operator means to get memory contents pointed to by the **pa** or **pb** pointer (also called pointer dereference):

```
*pb = *pb + *pa;
```

In assembly language, we use the instruction ADD for the "+" operator, but we cannot use memory addresses in one step instruction:

```
add [x1], [x0]      // invalid instruction
```

We can only use registers, and, therefore, we need to employ two registers as temporary variables:

```
RegisterA <- [X0]
RegisterB <- [X1]
RegisterC <- RegisterB + RegisterA
[X1] <- RegisterC
```

We cannot use W0 and W1 to hold values since they are contained in X0 and X1; the addresses would be overwritten, so we use W2, W3, and W4. In assembly language, we write this sequence of instructions:

```
ldr   w2, [x0]
ldr   w3, [x1]
add   w4, w3, w2
str   w4, [x1]
```

In the GDB disassembly output, we see these instructions indeed:

```
0x00000000004000c4 <+20>:    ldr    w2, [x0]
0x00000000004000c8 <+24>:    ldr    w3, [x1]
0x00000000004000cc <+28>:    add    w4, w3, w2
0x00000000004000d0 <+32>:    str    w4, [x1]
```

We add them to our pseudo-code table:

X0 <- address a		adr x0, 0x4100f0
		mov w3, #0x1
[X0] <- 1	// [a] = 1	str w3, [x0]
X1 <- address b		adr x1, 0x4100f4
[X1] <- 1	// [b] = 1	str w3, [x1]
[X1] <- [X1] + [X0]	**// [b] = 2**	**ldr w2, [x0]**
		ldr w3, [x1]
		add w4, w3, w2
		str w4, [x1]
[X0] <- [X0] + 1		
[X1] <- [X1] * [X0]		

Now we execute these four instructions (we remind that the output of the **si** command shows the next instruction to be executed when we use the **si** command again):

[From the previous output]
```
8: /x (int)b = 0x1
7: /x (int)a = 0x1
6: /x $w4 = 0x0
5: /x $w3 = 0x1
4: /x $w2 = 0x0
3: /x $x1 = 0x4100f4
2: /x $x0 = 0x4100f0
1: x/i $pc
=> 0x4000c4 <main+20>:   ldr     w2, [x0]
(gdb) si
0x00000000004000c8 in main ()
8: /x (int)b = 0x1
7: /x (int)a = 0x1
6: /x $w4 = 0x0
5: /x $w3 = 0x1
```

4: /x $w2 = 0x1

3: /x $x1 = 0x4100f4

2: /x $x0 = 0x4100f0

1: x/i $pc

=> 0x4000c8 <main+24>:   ldr   w3, [x1]

(gdb) si

0x00000000004000cc in main ()

8: /x (int)b = 0x1

7: /x (int)a = 0x1

6: /x $w4 = 0x0

5: /x $w3 = 0x1

4: /x $w2 = 0x1

3: /x $x1 = 0x4100f4

2: /x $x0 = 0x4100f0

1: x/i $pc

=> 0x4000cc <main+28>:   add   w4, w3, w2

(gdb) si

0x00000000004000d0 in main ()

8: /x (int)b = 0x1

7: /x (int)a = 0x1

6: /x $w4 = 0x2

5: /x $w3 = 0x1

4: /x $w2 = 0x1

3: /x $x1 = 0x4100f4

2: /x $x0 = 0x4100f0

1: x/i $pc

=> 0x4000d0 <main+32>:   str   w4, [x1]

(gdb) si

0x00000000004000d4 in main ()

8: /x (int)b = 0x2

7: /x (int)a = 0x1

```
6: /x $w4 = 0x2
5: /x $w3 = 0x1
4: /x $w2 = 0x1
3: /x $x1 = 0x4100f4
2: /x $x0 = 0x4100f0
1: x/i $pc
=> 0x4000d4 <main+36>:   add     w2, w2, #0x1
```

All this corresponds to a memory layout shown in Figure 4-4.

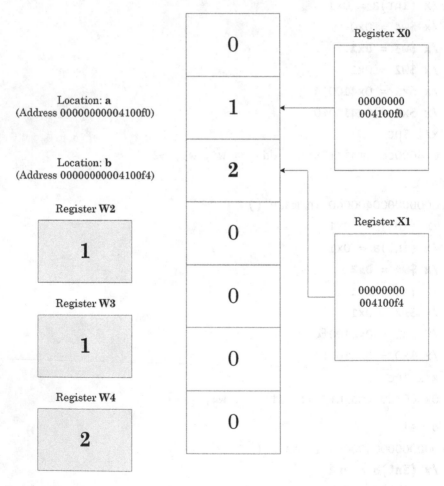

Figure 4-4. *Memory layout after executing the next four instructions*

Incrementing Numbers Using Pointers

In pseudo-code, it means increment (decrement) a number stored at the memory location which address is stored in X0:

```
[X0] <- [X0] + 1
```

In the C or C++ language, we can write this using three possible ways:

```
*a = *a + 1;
++(*a);
(*a)++;
```

In assembly language, we use instructions LDR, ADD, and STR and write

```
ldr  w2, [x0]     // this can be omitted since we already
                        loaded w2 previously
add  w2, w2, #0x1
str  w2, [x0]
```

In the GDB disassembly output, we see the same instructions:

```
0x00000000004000d4 <+36>:    add    w2, w2, #0x1
0x00000000004000d8 <+40>:    str    w2, [x0]
```

Now we add the assembly language translation of increment:

```
X0 <- address a                            adr  x0, 0x4100f0
                                           mov  w3, #0x1
[X0] <- 1                 // [a] = 1        str  w3, [x0]
X1 <- address b                            adr  x1, 0x4100f4
[X1] <- 1                 // [b] = 1        str  w3, [x1]
[X1] <- [X1] + [X0]       // [b] = 2        ldr  w2, [x0]
                                           ldr  w3, [x1]
                                           add  w4, w3, w2
                                           str  w4, [x1]
[X0] <- [X0] + 1          // [a] = 2        add  w2, w2, #0x1
                                           str  w2, [x0]
[X1] <- [X1] * [X0]
```

Now we execute these two instructions (we remind that the output of
the **si** command shows the next instruction to be executed when we use
the **si** command again):

[From the previous output]

```
8: /x (int)b = 0x2
7: /x (int)a = 0x1
6: /x $w4 = 0x2
5: /x $w3 = 0x1
4: /x $w2 = 0x1
3: /x $x1 = 0x4100f4
2: /x $x0 = 0x4100f0
1: x/i $pc
=> 0x4000d4 <main+36>:  add     w2, w2, #0x1

(gdb) si
0x00000000004000d8 in main ()
8: /x (int)b = 0x2
7: /x (int)a = 0x1
```

```
6: /x $w4 = 0x2
5: /x $w3 = 0x1
4: /x $w2 = 0x2
3: /x $x1 = 0x4100f4
2: /x $x0 = 0x4100f0
1: x/i $pc
=> 0x4000d8 <main+40>:    str      w2, [x0]

(gdb) si
0x00000000004000dc in main ()
8: /x (int)b = 0x2
7: /x (int)a = 0x2
6: /x $w4 = 0x2
5: /x $w3 = 0x1
4: /x $w2 = 0x2
3: /x $x1 = 0x4100f4
2: /x $x0 = 0x4100f0
1: x/i $pc
=> 0x4000dc <main+44>:    mul      w3, w4, w2
```

After the execution of ADD and STR instructions, we have the memory layout illustrated in Figure 4-5.

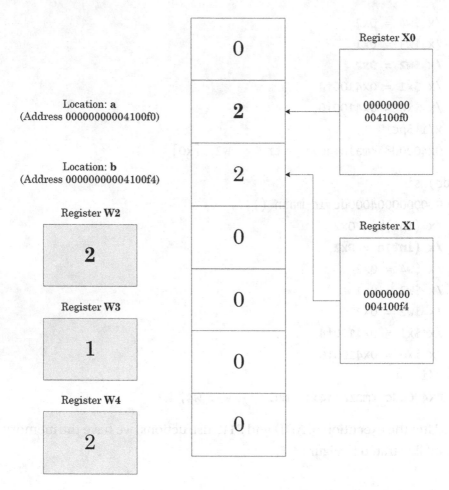

Figure 4-5. *Memory layout after the execution of ADD and STR instructions*

Multiplying Numbers Using Pointers

Our next pseudo-code statement does multiplication:

[X1] <- [X1] * [X0]

This statement means that we multiply the contents of the memory cell whose address is stored in the X1 register by the value stored in the memory cell whose address is in the X0 register. In the C or C++ language, we write a similar expression as the addition statement we have seen in the previous sections (note that we have two distinct meanings of the "*" operator: pointer dereference and multiplication):

```
*pb = *pb * *pa;
*pb *= *pa;
```

The latter is a shorthand notation. In assembly language, we use instruction MUL and registers that hold values to multiply. Registers W2 and W4 already hold values from [X0] and [X1] from the previous code, so we don't need load instructions, but we use W3 to hold the multiplication result:

```
mul   w3, w4, w2
str   w3, [x1]
```

In the GDB disassembly output, we see this:

```
0x00000000004000dc <+44>:    mul    w3, w4, w2
0x00000000004000e0 <+48>:    str    w3, [x1]
```

We add instructions to our pseudo-code table:

```
X0 <- address a                          adr   x0, 0x4100f0
                                         mov   w3, #0x1
[X0] <- 1                // [a] = 1      str   w3, [x0]
X1 <- address b                          adr   x1, 0x4100f4
[X1] <- 1                // [b] = 1      str   w3, [x1]
[X1] <- [X1] + [X0]      // [b] = 2      ldr   w2, [x0]
                                         ldr   w3, [x1]
                                         add   w4, w3, w2
                                         str   w4, [x1]
[X0] <- [X0] + 1         // [a] = 2      add   w2, w2, #0x1
                                         str   w2, [x0]
[X1] <- [X1] * [X0]      // [b] = 4      mul   w3, w4, w2
                                         str   w3, [x1]
```

Now we execute these two instructions (we remind that the output of
the **si** command shows the next instruction to be executed when we use
the **si** command again):

[From the previous output]

```
8: /x (int)b = 0x2
7: /x (int)a = 0x2
6: /x $w4 = 0x2
5: /x $w3 = 0x1
4: /x $w2 = 0x2
3: /x $x1 = 0x4100f4
2: /x $x0 = 0x4100f0
1: x/i $pc
=> 0x4000dc <main+44>:  mul     w3, w4, w2

(gdb) si
8: /x (int)b = 0x2
7: /x (int)a = 0x2
```

```
6: /x $w4 = 0x2
5: /x $w3 = 0x4
4: /x $w2 = 0x2
3: /x $x1 = 0x4100f4
2: /x $x0 = 0x4100f0
1: x/i $pc
=> 0x4000e0 <main+48>:  str     w3, [x1]

(gdb) si
0x00000000004000e4 in main ()
8: /x (int)b = 0x4
7: /x (int)a = 0x2
6: /x $w4 = 0x2
5: /x $w3 = 0x4
4: /x $w2 = 0x2
3: /x $x1 = 0x4100f4
2: /x $x0 = 0x4100f0
1: x/i $pc
=> 0x4000e4 <main+52>:  mov     x0, #0x0                  // #0
```

All this corresponds to a memory layout shown in Figure 4-6.

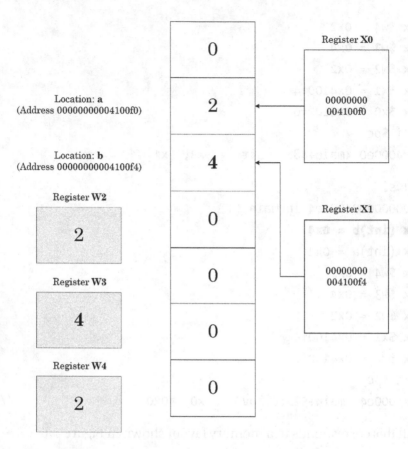

Figure 4-6. *Memory layout after execution of the last two instructions*

Summary

This chapter introduced pointers. We rewrote our arithmetic program from Chapter 1 using pointers, used the GDB debugger to execute instructions individually, and watched changes to memory. We also learned GDB commands to show the contents of registers and variables.

The next chapter introduces the bit- and byte-level memory granularity, corresponding layout, and integral C and C++ types.

CHAPTER 5

Bytes, Halfwords, Words, and Doublewords

Using Hexadecimal Numbers

If we want to use hexadecimal numbers in the C/C++ language, we prefix them with **0x**, for example:

```
a = 12;    // 12_dec
a = 0xC;   // C_hex
```

In the GDB disassembly output, and when entering commands, numbers are interpreted as decimals by default. If we want a number to be interpreted as hexadecimal, we prefix it with **0x**, for example:

```
mov  X0, #12
mov  X0, #0xC
```

© Dmitry Vostokov 2023

D. Vostokov, *Foundations of ARM64 Linux Debugging, Disassembling, and Reversing*,
https://doi.org/10.1007/978-1-4842-9082-8_5

Byte Granularity

Figure 5-1 shows the difference between bytes, halfwords, words, and doublewords in terms of byte granularity. We see that each successive size is double the previous.

Byte	Byte							
Halfword	Byte	Byte						
Word	Byte	Byte	Byte	Byte				
Doubleword	Byte	Byte	Byte	Byte	Byte	Byte	Byte	Byte

Figure 5-1. *Difference between bytes, halfwords, words, and doublewords*

Bit Granularity

Every byte consists of eight bits. Every bit has a value of zero or one. Here are some examples of bytes, halfwords, words, and doublewords shown as bit strings (we can also clearly see the correspondence between 4-bit sequences and hexadecimal numbers, Table 3-1):

- Byte

  C/C++: unsigned char

  8 bits

  Values 0_{dec}–255_{dec} or 0_{hex}–FF_{hex}

  Example: 12_{dec} 00001100_{bin} $0C_{hex}$

- Halfword

  C/C++: unsigned short

16 bits

Values 0_{dec}–65535_{dec} or 0_{hex}–$FFFF_{hex}$

Example: 0000000000001100_{bin} $000C_{hex}$

- Word

  C/C++: unsigned int, unsigned

  32 bits

  Values 0_{dec}–4294967295_{dec} or 0_{hex}–$FFFFFFFF_{hex}$

  Example: $00000000000000000000000000001100_{bin}$

  $0000000C_{hex}$

- Doubleword

  C/C++: long, unsigned long long

  64 bits

  Values 0_{dec}–$18446744073709551615_{dec}$ or

  0_{hex}–$FFFFFFFFFFFFFFFF_{hex}$

  Example: $0000000000000000000000000000000000000000000000000000000000001100_{bin}$

  $000000000000000C_{hex}$

Memory Layout

The minimum addressable element of memory is a byte. The maximum addressable element is a word on 32-bit machines and a doubleword on 64-bit machines. All general registers are 32-bit on 32-bit CPUs and can contain word values. On 64-bit CPUs, all general registers are 64-bit and can contain doubleword values. Figure 5-2 shows a typical memory layout, and Figure 5-3 shows the byte layout of some general CPU registers.

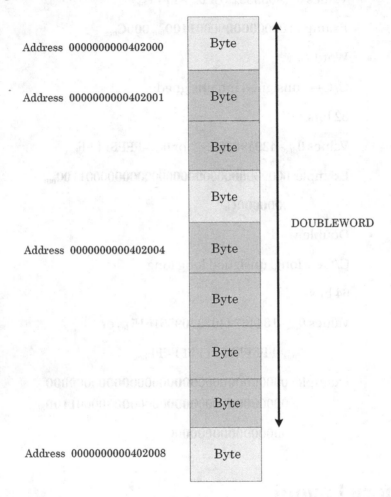

Figure 5-2. *Typical memory layout*

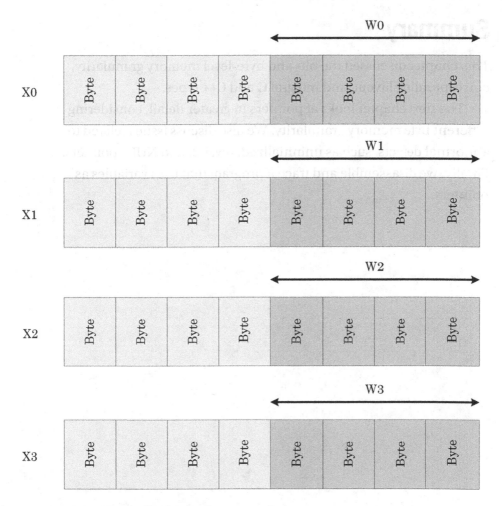

Figure 5-3. *Typical registry layout*

Remember that memory addresses are always 64-bit, and memory addresses to 32-bit memory cells like integers are also 64-bit.

Summary

This chapter discussed the bit- and byte-level memory granularity, corresponding layout, and integral C and C++ types.

The next chapter looks at pointers in greater detail, considering different byte memory granularity. We also discuss issues related to abnormal defects, such as uninitialized, invalid, and NULL pointers. Finally, we disassemble and trace a program that uses variables as pointers.

CHAPTER 6

Pointers to Memory

Pointers Revisited

The pointer is a memory cell or a register that contains the address of another memory cell. Memory pointers have their own addresses because they are memory cells too. On 32-bit Linux, pointers are 32-bit, and on 64-bit Linux, pointers are 64-bit.

Addressing Types

As we have seen in Chapter 5, memory cells can be of one byte, halfword, word, or doubleword size. Therefore, we can have a pointer to a byte, a pointer to a halfword, a pointer to a word, and a pointer to a doubleword. If we want to load or store a byte, we use LDRB/STRB and W-registers for data, a halfword – LDRH/STRH and W-registers for data, a word – LDR/STR and W-registers for data, a doubleword – LDR/STR and X-registers for data. We always use X-registers for memory addresses.

Here are some illustrated examples:

```
mov  w1, #0xFF
ldrb w1, [x0]            // load one byte
strb w1, [x0]            // stores one byte
str  w1, [x0]            // stores one word
ldr  x1, [x0]            // loads one doubleword
```

© Dmitry Vostokov 2023
D. Vostokov, *Foundations of ARM64 Linux Debugging, Disassembling, and Reversing*,
https://doi.org/10.1007/978-1-4842-9082-8_6

We prefix 0xFF with the # sign to differentiate it from 0xFF as a memory address. The layout of memory before **strb** instruction execution is shown in Figure 6-1, and the layout of memory after execution is shown in Figure 6-2.

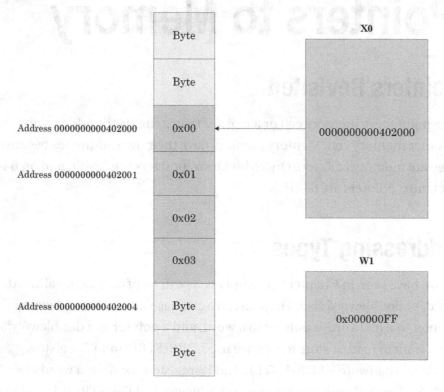

Figure 6-1. *The layout of memory before **strb** instruction execution*

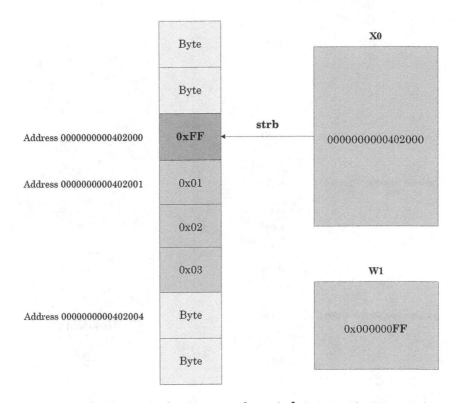

Figure 6-2. *The layout of memory after* **strb** *instruction execution*

The layout of memory after the execution of the **str** instruction is shown in Figure 6-3. The instruction replaces all 4 bytes of a word in memory because we specify the destination as 4 bytes (W1 source register) and 0xFF is 0x000000FF as a word. It is stored as FF 00 00 00 sequence of bytes in memory (little-endian system).

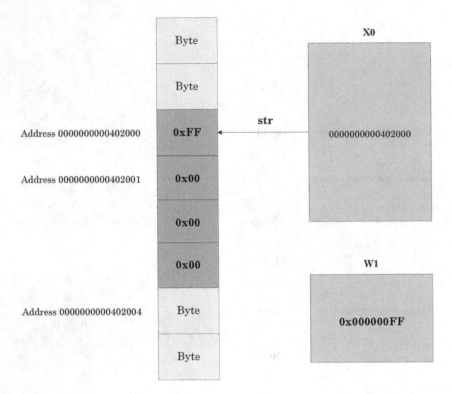

Figure 6-3. *The layout of memory after the execution of* **str** *instruction*

Figure 6-4 shows a summary of various addressing modes.

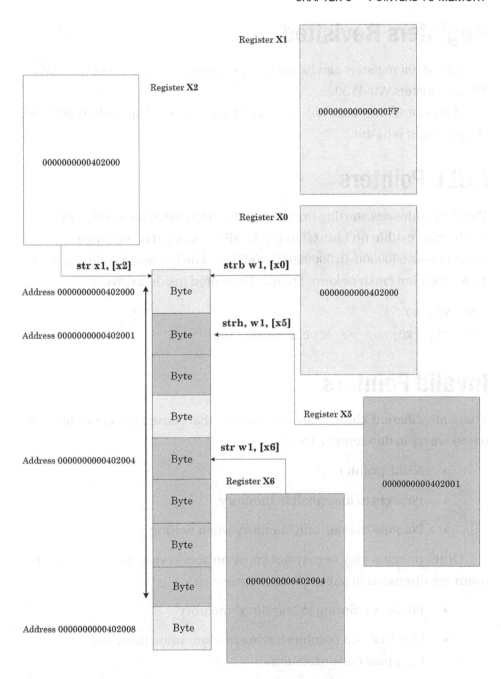

Figure 6-4. *A summary of various addressing modes*

Registers Revisited

X0–X30 64-bit registers can be used as pointers to memory. They contain 32-bit registers W0–W30.

If an instruction uses W0–W30 registers, the size of operations is 32-bit. Otherwise, it is 64-bit.

NULL Pointers

The first addresses starting from 0x0000000000000000 are specifically made inaccessible on Linux. On my ARM64 system, it is the range 0x0000000000000000–0x0000000000007FFF. The following code will force an application crash or kernel panic if executed inside a driver:

```
mov  x0, #0
str  x1, [x0]      // Access violation
```

Invalid Pointers

There are different kinds of invalid pointers that cause an access violation when we try to dereference them:

- NULL pointers

- Pointers to inaccessible memory

- Pointers to read-only memory when writing

Other pointers may or may not cause an access violation, and some of them are discussed in subsequent chapters:

- Pointers pointing to "random" memory

- Uninitialized pointers having random value inherited from past code execution

- Dangling pointers

The latter pointers are similar to pointers pointing to "random" memory locations and arise when we forget to set pointer variables to zero (NULL) after disposing of the memory they point to. By nullifying pointers, we indicate that they no longer point to memory.

Variables As Pointers

Suppose we have two memory addresses (locations) "a" and "b" declared and defined in C and C++ as

```
int a, b;
```

These are normal variables "a" and "b." Also, we can have another two memory addresses (locations) "pa" and "pb" declared and defined in C and C++ as

```
int *pa, *pb;
```

Here, **pa** is a pointer to an int, or, in other words, the memory cell **pa** contains the address of another memory cell that contains an integer value.

Pointer Initialization

In order to have pointers to point to memory, we need to initialize them with corresponding memory addresses. Here is a typical C or C++ code that does what we need:

```
int a;              // uninitialized variable
int *pa;            // uninitialized pointer
pa = &a;            // (pa) now contains the address a
int b = 12;         // initialized variable
int *pb = &b;       // initialized pointer
```

We see that pointers are also variables and can change their values effectively pointing to different memory locations during program execution.

Initialized and Uninitialized Data

Here is a bit of additional information about initialized and uninitialized variables that is useful to know: an executable program in Linux is divided into different sections. One is called **.data**, where all global and static variables (including pointers) are put.

Consider this C or C++ data definition:

```
int array[1000000]; // size 4,000,000 bytes or 3.8Mb
```

We would expect the size of an executable file to be about 4Mb. However, the program size on a disk is only 16Kb. It is because the uninitialized array contains only information about its size. When we launch the program, this array is recreated from its size information and filled with zeroes. The size of the program in memory becomes about 4Mb.

In the case of the initialized array, the program size on disk is 4.01Mb:

```
int array[1000000] = { 12 };
```

This is because the array was put into a .data section and contains the following sequence of integers { 12, 0, 0, 0, 0 ... }.

More Pseudo Notation

We remind that **[a]** means contents of memory at the address **a**, and **[x0]** means contents of a 32-bit or 64-bit memory cell at the address stored in the X0 register (here, X0 is a pointer).

We also introduce an additional notation to employ in this and subsequent chapters: ***[pa]** means contents at the address stored at the address **pa** and is called dereferencing a pointer whose address is **pa**. The corresponding C/C++ code is similar:

```
int *pa = &a;
int b = *pa;
```

"MemoryPointers" Project: Memory Layout

This project is very similar to the "Pointers" project from Chapter 4. We have the following data declaration and definition in the C or C++ language:

```
int a, b;
int *pa, *pb = &b;
```

The project code corresponds to the following pseudo-code and assembly language:

```
[pa] <- address a                        adr  x0, a
                                         adr  x1, pa
                                         str  x0, [x1]
*[pa] <- 1               ; [a] = 1       adr  x0, pa
                                         ldr  x0, [x0]
                                         mov  w2, #1
                                         str  w2, [x0]
*[pb] <- 1               ; [b] = 1       adr  x1, pb
                                         ldr  x1, [x1]
                                         str  w2, [x1]
*[pb] <- *[pb] + *[pa]   ; [b] = 2       ldr  w2, [x0]
                                         ldr  w3, [x1]
                                         add  w3, w3, w2
                                         str  w3, [x1]
```

The source code for this chapter can be downloaded from
github.com/apress/arm64-linux-debugging-disassembling-reversing/
Chapter6/

We compile and link it and load the executable into GDB as described
in Chapter 4. We get the following output:

```
$ as MemoryPointers.asm -o MemoryPointers.o

$ ld MemoryPointers.o -o MemoryPointers

$ gdb ./MemoryPointers
GNU gdb (GDB) Red Hat Enterprise Linux 7.6.1-120.0.2.el7
Copyright (C) 2013 Free Software Foundation, Inc.
License GPLv3+: GNU GPL version 3 or later <http://gnu.org/
licenses/gpl.html>
This is free software: you are free to change and
redistribute it.
```

There is NO WARRANTY, to the extent permitted by law. Type
"show copying"
and "show warranty" for details.
This GDB was configured as "aarch64-redhat-linux-gnu".
For bug reporting instructions, please see:
<http://www.gnu.org/software/gdb/bugs/>...
Reading symbols from /home/crashdump/pflddr/A64/Chapter6/
MemoryPointers...(no debugging symbols found)...done.
(gdb)

Then we put a breakpoint on the *main* function and run the program
until GDB breaks in:

```
(gdb) break main
Breakpoint 1 at 0x4000b0

(gdb) run
Starting program: /home/crashdump/pflddr/A64/Chapter6/./
MemoryPointers

Breakpoint 1, 0x00000000004000b0 in main ()
```

We disassemble the *main* function:

```
(gdb) disass main
Dump of assembler code for function main:
=> 0x00000000004000b0 <+0>:      adr     x0, 0x4100f4
   0x00000000004000b4 <+4>:      adr     x1, 0x4100fc
   0x00000000004000b8 <+8>:      str     x0, [x1]
   0x00000000004000bc <+12>:     adr     x0, 0x4100fc
   0x00000000004000c0 <+16>:     ldr     x0, [x0]
   0x00000000004000c4 <+20>:     mov     w2, #0x1          // #1
   0x00000000004000c8 <+24>:     str     w2, [x0]
   0x00000000004000cc <+28>:     adr     x1, 0x410104
```

```
0x00000000004000d0 <+32>:     ldr     x1, [x1]
0x00000000004000d4 <+36>:     str     w2, [x1]
0x00000000004000d8 <+40>:     ldr     w2, [x0]
0x00000000004000dc <+44>:     ldr     w3, [x1]
0x00000000004000e0 <+48>:     add     w3, w3, w2
0x00000000004000e4 <+52>:     str     w3, [x1]
0x00000000004000e8 <+56>:     mov     x0, #0x0        // #0
0x00000000004000ec <+60>:     mov     w8, #0x5d       // #93
0x00000000004000f0 <+64>:     svc     #0x0
```
End of assembler dump.

Then we clear X0–X3 registers to set up a memory layout that is easy to follow:

```
(gdb) set $x0 = 0

(gdb) set $x1 = 0

(gdb) set $x2 = 0

(gdb) set $x3 = 0

(gdb) info registers x0 x1 x2 x3
x0              0x0        0
x1              0x0        0
x2              0x0        0
x3              0x0        0
```

We also instruct GDB to automatically display the current instruction to be executed, the values of registers X0–X3, and the contents of variables "a," "b," "pa," and "pb":

```
(gdb) display/i $pc
1: x/i $pc
=> 0x4000b0 <main>:      adr      x0, 0x4100f4

(gdb) display/x $x0
2: /x $x0 = 0x0

(gdb) display/x $x1
3: /x $x1 = 0x0

(gdb) display/x $x2
4: /x $x2 = 0x0

(gdb) display/x $x3
5: /x $x3 = 0x0

(gdb) display/x (int)a
6: /x (int)a = 0x0

(gdb) display/x (int)b
7: /x (int)b = 0x0

(gdb) display/x (long)pa
8: /x (long)pa = 0x0

(gdb) display/x (long)pb
9: /x (long)pb = 0x4100f8
```

We see that the **pb** variable contains the address 0x4100f8. We then check the addresses of (variables) memory locations "a," "b," "pa," and "pb":

```
(gdb) print &a
$1 = (<data variable, no debug info> *) 0x4100f4

(gdb) print &b
$2 = (<data variable, no debug info> *) 0x4100f8
```

```
(gdb) print &pa
$3 = (<data variable, no debug info> *) 0x4100fc

(gdb) print &pb
$4 = (<data variable, no debug info> *) 0x410104
```

We also check the value stored at the address 0x4100f8 (value of **pb** that is the address of **b**):

```
(gdb) x 0x4100f8
0x4100f8:          0x00000000
```

This output corresponds to the memory layout before executing the first ADR instruction, and it is shown in Figure 6-5.

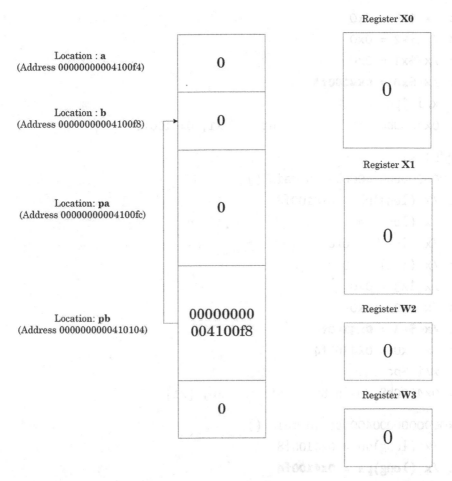

Figure 6-5. *Memory layout before executing the first ADR instruction*

We then execute our code step by step (changes are in bold):

```
(gdb) si
0x00000000004000b4 in main ()
9: /x (long)pb = 0x4100f8
8: /x (long)pa = 0x0
7: /x (int)b = 0x0
6: /x (int)a = 0x0
```

```
5: /x $x3 = 0x0
4: /x $x2 = 0x0
3: /x $x1 = 0x0
2: /x $x0 = 0x4100f4
1: x/i $pc
=> 0x4000b4 <main+4>:    adr     x1, 0x4100fc

(gdb) si
0x00000000004000b8 in main ()
9: /x (long)pb = 0x4100f8
8: /x (long)pa = 0x0
7: /x (int)b = 0x0
6: /x (int)a = 0x0
5: /x $x3 = 0x0
4: /x $x2 = 0x0
3: /x $x1 = 0x4100fc
2: /x $x0 = 0x4100f4
1: x/i $pc
=> 0x4000b8 <main+8>:    str     x0, [x1]

0x00000000004000bc in main ()
9: /x (long)pb = 0x4100f8
8: /x (long)pa = 0x4100f4
7: /x (int)b = 0x0
6: /x (int)a = 0x0
5: /x $x3 = 0x0
4: /x $x2 = 0x0
3: /x $x1 = 0x4100fc
2: /x $x0 = 0x4100f4
1: x/i $pc
=> 0x4000bc <main+12>:   adr     x0, 0x4100fc

(gdb) si
```

```
0x00000000004000c0 in main ()
9: /x (long)pb = 0x4100f8
8: /x (long)pa = 0x4100f4
7: /x (int)b = 0x0
6: /x (int)a = 0x0
5: /x $x3 = 0x0
4: /x $x2 = 0x0
3: /x $x1 = 0x4100fc
2: /x $x0 = 0x4100fc
1: x/i $pc
=> 0x4000c0 <main+16>:  ldr     x0, [x0]

(gdb) si
0x00000000004000c4 in main ()
9: /x (long)pb = 0x4100f8
8: /x (long)pa = 0x4100f4
7: /x (int)b = 0x0
6: /x (int)a = 0x0
5: /x $x3 = 0x0
4: /x $x2 = 0x0
3: /x $x1 = 0x4100fc
2: /x $x0 = 0x4100f4
1: x/i $pc
=> 0x4000c4 <main+20>:  mov     w2,
#0x1                            // #1

(gdb) si
0x00000000004000c8 in main ()
9: /x (long)pb = 0x4100f8
8: /x (long)pa = 0x4100f4
7: /x (int)b = 0x0
6: /x (int)a = 0x0
```

```
5: /x $x3 = 0x0
4: /x $x2 = 0x1
3: /x $x1 = 0x4100fc
2: /x $x0 = 0x4100f4
1: x/i $pc
=> 0x4000c8 <main+24>:   str     w2, [x0]

(gdb) si
0x00000000004000cc in main ()
9: /x (long)pb = 0x4100f8
8: /x (long)pa = 0x4100f4
7: /x (int)b = 0x0
6: /x (int)a = 0x1
5: /x $x3 = 0x0
4: /x $x2 = 0x1
3: /x $x1 = 0x4100fc
2: /x $x0 = 0x4100f4
1: x/i $pc
=> 0x4000cc <main+28>:   adr     x1, 0x410104

(gdb) si
0x00000000004000d0 in main ()
9: /x (long)pb = 0x4100f8
8: /x (long)pa = 0x4100f4
7: /x (int)b = 0x0
6: /x (int)a = 0x1
5: /x $x3 = 0x0
4: /x $x2 = 0x1
3: /x $x1 = 0x410104
2: /x $x0 = 0x4100f4
1: x/i $pc
=> 0x4000d0 <main+32>:   ldr     x1, [x1]
```

```
(gdb) si
0x00000000004000d4 in main ()
9: /x (long)pb = 0x4100f8
8: /x (long)pa = 0x4100f4
7: /x (int)b = 0x0
6: /x (int)a = 0x1
5: /x $x3 = 0x0
4: /x $x2 = 0x1
3: /x $x1 = 0x4100f8
2: /x $x0 = 0x4100f4
1: x/i $pc
=> 0x4000d4 <main+36>:   str     w2, [x1]

(gdb) si
0x00000000004000d8 in main ()
9: /x (long)pb = 0x4100f8
8: /x (long)pa = 0x4100f4
7: /x (int)b = 0x1
6: /x (int)a = 0x1
5: /x $x3 = 0x0
4: /x $x2 = 0x1
3: /x $x1 = 0x4100f8
2: /x $x0 = 0x4100f4
1: x/i $pc
=> 0x4000d8 <main+40>:   ldr     w2, [x0]

(gdb) si
0x00000000004000dc in main ()
9: /x (long)pb = 0x4100f8
8: /x (long)pa = 0x4100f4
7: /x (int)b = 0x1
6: /x (int)a = 0x1
```

```
5: /x $x3 = 0x0
4: /x $x2 = 0x1
3: /x $x1 = 0x4100f8
2: /x $x0 = 0x4100f4
1: x/i $pc
=> 0x4000dc <main+44>:  ldr     w3, [x1]

(gdb) si
0x00000000004000e0 in main ()
9: /x (long)pb = 0x4100f8
8: /x (long)pa = 0x4100f4
7: /x (int)b = 0x1
6: /x (int)a = 0x1
5: /x $x3 = 0x1
4: /x $x2 = 0x1
3: /x $x1 = 0x4100f8
2: /x $x0 = 0x4100f4
1: x/i $pc
=> 0x4000e0 <main+48>:  add     w3, w3, w2

(gdb) si
0x00000000004000e4 in main ()
9: /x (long)pb = 0x4100f8
8: /x (long)pa = 0x4100f4
7: /x (int)b = 0x1
6: /x (int)a = 0x1
5: /x $x3 = 0x2
4: /x $x2 = 0x1
3: /x $x1 = 0x4100f8
2: /x $x0 = 0x4100f4
1: x/i $pc
=> 0x4000e4 <main+52>:  str     w3, [x1]
```

```
(gdb) si
0x00000000004000e8 in main ()
9: /x (long)pb = 0x4100f8
8: /x (long)pa = 0x4100f4
7: /x (int)b = 0x2
6: /x (int)a = 0x1
5: /x $x3 = 0x2
4: /x $x2 = 0x1
3: /x $x1 = 0x4100f8
2: /x $x0 = 0x4100f4
1: x/i $pc
=> 0x4000e8 <main+56>:    mov      x0, #0x0                    // #0
```

The final memory layout and registers are shown in Figure 6-6.

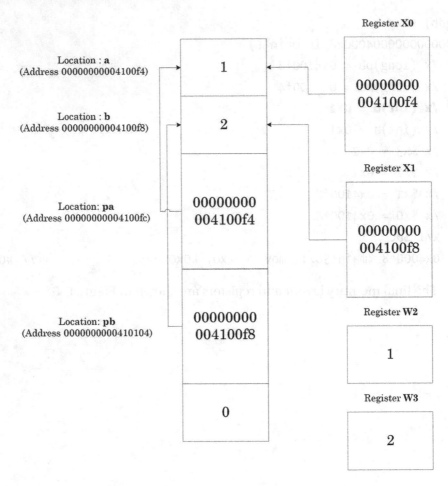

Figure 6-6. *The final memory layout and registers*

Summary

This chapter looked at pointers in greater detail, considering different byte memory granularity. We also discussed issues related to abnormal defects, such as uninitialized, invalid, and NULL pointers. Finally, in the GDB debugger, we disassembled and traced a program that used variables as pointers and learned additional commands to display memory addresses and contents.

The next chapter introduces logical instructions, the zero register, and the program counter register. We also learn an additional GDB command to get program code and data section addresses.

CHAPTER 7

Logical Instructions and PC

Instruction Format

We have seen that most assembly language instructions have a uniform format, for example:

Opcode *operand*
Opcode *destination_operand, source_operand*
Opcode *destination_operand, source_operand1, source_operand2*

STR-family of instructions have this format:

Opcode *source_operand, destination_operand*

Operands can be registers (reg), memory labels (mem), or some numbers, called immediate values (imm). Typical notational examples:

```
add   reg, reg, reg
add   reg, reg, imm
mov   reg, imm
adr   reg, mem
ldr   reg, [reg]
str   reg, [reg]
```

© Dmitry Vostokov 2023
D. Vostokov, *Foundations of ARM64 Linux Debugging, Disassembling, and Reversing*,
https://doi.org/10.1007/978-1-4842-9082-8_7

and some concrete assembly language examples:

```
add   w0, w1, w2
str   x0, [x1]
adr   x1, a
ldr   w4, [x8]
mov   w7, #2
```

Logical Shift Instructions

In addition to arithmetic instructions, there are so-called logical shift instructions that just shift a bit string to the left or the right.

Shift to the left:

```
11111110   <-   11111111          ; shift by 1
11110000   <-   11111110          ; shift by 3
lsl  regDst, regSrc, regShiftValue
mov  x0, #3
lsl  X2, X1, X0
```

Shift to the right:

```
01111111   <-   11111111          ; shift by 1
00001111   <-   01111111          ; shift by 3
lsr  regDst, regSrc, regShiftValue
mov  x0, #3
lsr  X2, X1, X0
```

Logical Operations

Here, we recall logical operations and corresponding truth tables. We abbreviate True as T and False as F.

AND

```
1 and 1 = 1     T and T = T
1 and 0 = 0     T and F = F
0 and 1 = 0     F and T = F
0 and 0 = 0     F and F = F
```

```
    OR
```

```
1 or 1 = 1      T or T = T
1 or 0 = 1      T or F = T
0 or 1 = 1      F or T = T
0 or 0 = 0      F or F = F
```

Zeroing Memory or Registers

There are several ways to put a zero value into a register or a memory location:

1. Move a value to a register:

   ```
   mov  x0, #0
   mov  w1, #0
   ```

2. Use the XOR (Exclusive OR) logical operation:

   ```
   eor regDst, regSrc1, regSrc2
   eor x0, x0, x0
   ```

   XOR

```
1 xor 1 = 0     T xor T = F
1 xor 0 = 1     T xor F = T
0 xor 1 = 1     F xor T = T
0 xor 0 = 0     F xor F = F
```

This operation clears its destination operand because the source operands are the same, and the same bits are cleared.

1. Move a value from a zero register (XZR/WZR) to a register:

    ```
    mov  x0, xzr
    mov  w1, wzr
    ```

Program Counter

Consider these two execution steps from the previous chapter project:

```
(gdb) si
0x00000000004000dc in main ()
9: /x (long)pb = 0x4100f8
8: /x (long)pa = 0x4100f4
7: /x (int)b = 0x1
6: /x (int)a = 0x1
5: /x $x3 = 0x0
4: /x $x2 = 0x1
3: /x $x1 = 0x4100f8
2: /x $x0 = 0x4100f4
1: x/i $pc
=> 0x4000dc <main+44>:  ldr    w3, [x1]

(gdb) si
0x00000000004000e0 in main ()
9: /x (long)pb = 0x4100f8
8: /x (long)pa = 0x4100f4
7: /x (int)b = 0x1
6: /x (int)a = 0x1
5: /x $x3 = 0x1
```

```
4: /x $x2 = 0x1
3: /x $x1 = 0x4100f8
2: /x $x0 = 0x4100f4
1: x/i $pc
=> 0x4000e0 <main+48>:   add     w3, w3, w2
```

When the LDR instruction at the 00000000004000dc address is being
executed, another CPU register PC points to the next instruction at the
00000000004000e0 address to be executed. This output is shown in
Figure 7-1.

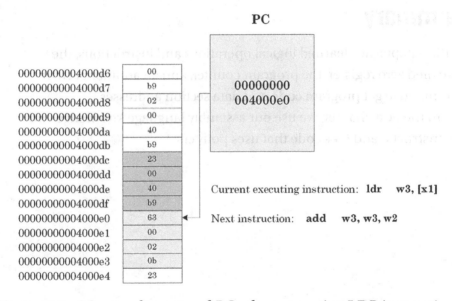

Figure 7-1. *Memory layout and PC when executing LDR instruction*

Code Section

Recall that in Chapter 6, we discussed the **.data** section where program
data is put. The program code is put into the **.text** section.

The following GDB command lists various program sections and their
information:

```
(gdb) maintenance info sections
Exec file:
    `/home/coredump/pflddr/A64/Chapter6/MemoryPointers', file
type elf64-littleaarch64.
    0x004000b0->0x004000f4 at 0x000000b0: .text ALLOC LOAD
READONLY CODE HAS_CONTENTS
    0x004100f4->0x0041010c at 0x000000f4: .data ALLOC LOAD DATA
HAS_CONTENTS
```

Summary

In this chapter, we learned logical operations and instructions, the so-called zero register, the program counter, and an additional GDB command to get program code and data section addresses.

In the next chapter, we use our assembly language knowledge and reconstruct C and C++ code that uses pointers.

CHAPTER 8

Reconstructing a Program with Pointers

Example of Disassembly Output: No Optimization

The ability to reconstruct approximate C or C++ code from code disassembly is essential in memory dump analysis and debugging.

The project for this chapter can be downloaded from
github.com/apress/arm64-linux-debugging-disassembling-reversing/ Chapter8/

We compile and link it, load executable into GDB, put a breakpoint on the *main* function, and run the program until GDB breaks in, then disassemble its *main* function:

```
$ gcc PointersAsVariables.cpp -o PointersAsVariables

$ gdb ./PointersAsVariables
GNU gdb (GDB) Red Hat Enterprise Linux 7.6.1-120.0.2.el7
Copyright (C) 2013 Free Software Foundation, Inc.
```

© Dmitry Vostokov 2023
D. Vostokov, *Foundations of ARM64 Linux Debugging, Disassembling, and Reversing*,
https://doi.org/10.1007/978-1-4842-9082-8_8

License GPLv3+: GNU GPL version 3 or later <http://gnu.org/licenses/gpl.html>
This is free software: you are free to change and redistribute it.
There is NO WARRANTY, to the extent permitted by law. Type "show copying"
and "show warranty" for details.
This GDB was configured as "aarch64-redhat-linux-gnu".
For bug reporting instructions, please see:
<http://www.gnu.org/software/gdb/bugs/>...
Reading symbols from /home/coredump/pflddr/A64/Chapter8/PointersAsVariables...(no debugging symbols found)...done.

(gdb) break main
Breakpoint 1 at 0x4005bc

(gdb) run
Starting program: /home/coredump/pflddr/A64/Chapter8/./PointersAsVariables

Breakpoint 1, 0x00000000004005bc in main ()
Missing separate debuginfos, use: debuginfo-install glibc-2.17-325.0.2.el7_9.aarch64

(gdb) disas main
Dump of assembler code for function main:
```
   0x00000000004005b8 <+0>:     sub     sp, sp, #0x10
=> 0x00000000004005bc <+4>:     str     w0, [sp,#12]
   0x00000000004005c0 <+8>:     str     x1, [sp]
   0x00000000004005c4 <+12>:    adrp    x0, 0x420000
   0x00000000004005c8 <+16>:    add     x0, x0, #0x30
   0x00000000004005cc <+20>:    adrp    x1, 0x420000
   0x00000000004005d0 <+24>:    add     x1, x1, #0x28
```

```
0x00000000004005d4 <+28>:    str     x1, [x0]
0x00000000004005d8 <+32>:    adrp    x0, 0x420000
0x00000000004005dc <+36>:    add     x0, x0, #0x38
0x00000000004005e0 <+40>:    adrp    x1, 0x420000
0x00000000004005e4 <+44>:    add     x1, x1, #0x2c
0x00000000004005e8 <+48>:    str     x1, [x0]
0x00000000004005ec <+52>:    adrp    x0, 0x420000
0x00000000004005f0 <+56>:    add     x0, x0, #0x30
0x00000000004005f4 <+60>:    ldr     x0, [x0]
0x00000000004005f8 <+64>:    mov     w1, #0x1        // #1
0x00000000004005fc <+68>:    str     w1, [x0]
0x0000000000400600 <+72>:    adrp    x0, 0x420000
0x0000000000400604 <+76>:    add     x0, x0, #0x38
0x0000000000400608 <+80>:    ldr     x0, [x0]
0x000000000040060c <+84>:    mov     w1, #0x1        // #1
0x0000000000400610 <+88>:    str     w1, [x0]
0x0000000000400614 <+92>:    adrp    x0, 0x420000
0x0000000000400618 <+96>:    add     x0, x0, #0x38
0x000000000040061c <+100>:   ldr     x0, [x0]
0x0000000000400620 <+104>:   adrp    x1, 0x420000
0x0000000000400624 <+108>:   add     x1, x1, #0x38
0x0000000000400628 <+112>:   ldr     x1, [x1]
0x000000000040062c <+116>:   ldr     w2, [x1]
0x0000000000400630 <+120>:   adrp    x1, 0x420000
0x0000000000400634 <+124>:   add     x1, x1, #0x30
0x0000000000400638 <+128>:   ldr     x1, [x1]
0x000000000040063c <+132>:   ldr     w1, [x1]
0x0000000000400640 <+136>:   add     w1, w2, w1
0x0000000000400644 <+140>:   str     w1, [x0]
```

```
---Type <return> to continue, or q <return> to quit---
   0x0000000000400648 <+144>:    adrp    x0, 0x420000
   0x000000000040064c <+148>:    add     x0, x0, #0x30
   0x0000000000400650 <+152>:    ldr     x0, [x0]
   0x0000000000400654 <+156>:    ldr     w1, [x0]
   0x0000000000400658 <+160>:    add     w1, w1, #0x1
   0x000000000040065c <+164>:    str     w1, [x0]
   0x0000000000400660 <+168>:    adrp    x0, 0x420000
   0x0000000000400664 <+172>:    add     x0, x0, #0x38
   0x0000000000400668 <+176>:    ldr     x0, [x0]
   0x000000000040066c <+180>:    adrp    x1, 0x420000
   0x0000000000400670 <+184>:    add     x1, x1, #0x38
   0x0000000000400674 <+188>:    ldr     x1, [x1]
   0x0000000000400678 <+192>:    ldr     w2, [x1]
   0x000000000040067c <+196>:    adrp    x1, 0x420000
   0x0000000000400680 <+200>:    add     x1, x1, #0x30
   0x0000000000400684 <+204>:    ldr     x1, [x1]
   0x0000000000400688 <+208>:    ldr     w1, [x1]
   0x000000000040068c <+212>:    mul     w1, w2, w1
   0x0000000000400690 <+216>:    str     w1, [x0]
   0x0000000000400694 <+220>:    mov     w0, #0x0                    // #0
   0x0000000000400698 <+224>:    add     sp, sp, #0x10
   0x000000000040069c <+228>:    ret
```

Reconstructing C/C++ Code: Part 1

Now we go from instruction to instruction highlighted in bold on the previous page and try to reconstruct pseudo-code which is shown as comments to assembly language code.

```
adrp    x0, 0x420000
add     x0, x0, #0x30        // x0 <- address var1 (0x420030)
adrp    x1, 0x420000         //
add     x1, x1, #0x28        // x1 <- address var2 (0x420028)
str     x1, [x0]             // [x0] <- x1
adrp    x0, 0x420000         //
add     x0, x0, #0x38        // x0 <- address var3 (0x420038)
adrp    x1, 0x420000
add     x1, x1, #0x2c        // x1 <- address var4 (0x42002c)
str     x1, [x0]             // [x0] <- x1
adrp    x0, 0x420000
add     x0, x0, #0x30        // x0 <- address var1 (0x420030)
ldr     x0, [x0]             // x0 <- [x0]
mov     w1, #0x1             // w1 <- 1
str     w1, [x0]             // [x0] <- w1
adrp    x0, 0x420000
add     x0, x0, #0x38        // x0 <- address var3 (0x420038)
ldr     x0, [x0]             // x0 <- [x0]
mov     w1, #0x1             // w1 <- 1
str     w1, [x0]             // [x0] <- w1
adrp    x0, 0x420000
add     x0, x0, #0x38        // x0 <- address var3 (0x420038)
ldr     x0, [x0]             // x0 <- [x0]
adrp    x1, 0x420000
add     x1, x1, #0x38        // x1 <- address var3 (0x420038)
ldr     x1, [x1]             // x1 <- [x1]
ldr     w2, [x1]             // w2 <- [x1]
adrp    x1, 0x420000
add     x1, x1, #0x30        // x1 <- address var1 (0x420030)
ldr     x1, [x1]             // x1 <- [x1]
ldr     w1, [x1]             // w1 <- [x1]
```

```
add     w1, w2, w1              // w1 <- w2 + w1
str     w1, [x0]                // [x0] <- w1
adrp    x0, 0x420000
add     x0, x0, #0x30           // x0 <- address var1 (0x420030)
ldr     x0, [x0]                // x0 <- [x0]
ldr     w1, [x0]                // w1 <- [x0]
add     w1, w1, #0x1            // w1 <- w1 + 1
str     w1, [x0]                // [x0] <- w1
adrp    x0, 0x420000
add     x0, x0, #0x38           // x0 <- address var3 (0x420038)
ldr     x0, [x0]                // x0 <- [x0]
adrp    x1, 0x420000
add     x1, x1, #0x38           // x1 <- address var3 (0x420038)
ldr     x1, [x1]                // x1 <- [x1]
ldr     w2, [x1]                // w2 <- [x1]
adrp    x1, 0x420000
add     x1, x1, #0x30           // x1 <- address var1 (0x420030)
ldr     x1, [x1]                // x1 <- [x1]
ldr     w1, [x1]                // w1 <- [x1]
mul     w1, w2, w1              // w1 <- w2 * w1
str     w1, [x0]                // [x0] <- w1
```

Reconstructing C/C++ Code: Part 2

Now we group pseudo-code together with possible mixed C/C++ and
assembly language equivalents:

```
x0 <- address var1 (0x420030)      // int *var1;
x1 <- address var2 (0x420028)      // int var2;
[x0] <- x1                         // var1 = &var2;

x0 <- address var3 (0x420038)      // int *var3;
```

100

```
x1 <- address var4 (0x42002c)        // int var4;
[x0] <- x1                           // var3 = &var4;

x0 <- address var1 (0x420030)        // x0 = &var1;
x0 <- [x0]                           // x0 = *(&var1) = var1;
w1 <- 1                              // w1 = 1;
[x0] <- w1                           // *var1 = w1;

x0 <- address var3 (0x420038)        // x0 = &var3;
x0 <- [x0]                           // x0 = *(&var3) = var3;
w1 <- 1                              // w1 = 1;
[x0] <- w1                           // *var3 = w1;

x0 <- address var3 (0x420038)
x0 <- [x0]                           // x0 = var3;
x1 <- address var3 (0x420038)
x1 <- [x1]                           // x1 = var3;
w2 <- [x1]                           // w2 = *var3;
x1 <- address var1 (0x420030)
x1 <- [x1]                           // x1 = var1;
w1 <- [x1]                           // w1 = *var1;
w1 <- w2 + w1                        // w1 = w2 + w1;
[x0] <- w1                           // *var3 = w1;

x0 <- address var1 (0x420030)
x0 <- [x0]                           // x0 = var1;
w1 <- [x0]                           // w1 = *var1;
w1 <- w1 + 1                         // ++w1;
[x0] <- w1                           // *var1 = w1;

x0 <- address var3 (0x420038)
x0 <- [x0]                           // x0 = var3;
x1 <- address var3 (0x420038)
x1 <- [x1]                           // x1 = var3;
```

```
w2 <- [x1]                              // w2 = *var3;
x1 <- address var1 (0x420030)
x1 <- [x1]                              // x1 = var1;
w1 <- [x1]                              // w1 = *var1;
w1 <- w2 * w1                           // w1 = w2 * w1;
[x0] <- w1                              // *var3 = w1;
```

Reconstructing C/C++ Code: Part 3

Next, we combine more mixed statements into C/C++ language code:

```
int *var1;
int var2;
var1 = &var2;

int *var3;
int var4;
var3 = &var4;

x0 = &var1;
x0 = *(&var1) = var1;
w1 = 1;
*var1 = w1;                   // *var1 = 1;

x0 = &var3;
x0 = *(&var3) = var3;
w1 = 1;
*var3 = w1;                   // *var3 = 1;

x0 = var3;
x1 = var3;
w2 = *var3;
x1 = var1;
```

```
w1 = *var1;
w1 = w2 + w1;
*var3 = w1;                          // *var3 = *var3 + *var1;

x0 = var1;
w1 = *var1;
++w1;
*var1 = w1;                          // ++*var1;

x0 = var3;
x1 = var3;
w2 = *var3;
x1 = var1;
w1 = *var1;
w1 = w2 * w1;
*var3 = w1;                          // *var3 = *var3 * *var1;
```

Reconstructing C/C++ Code: C/C++ Program

Finally, we have something that looks like a complete C/C++ code:

```
int *var1;                          // int *pa;
int var2;                           // int a;
var1 = &var2;                       // pa = &a;

int *var3;                          // int *pb;
int var4;                           // int b;
var3 = &var4;                       // pb = &b;

*var1 = 1;                          // *pa = 1;

*var3 = 1;                          // *pb = 1;
```

```
*var3 = *var3 + *var1;          // *pb = *pb + *pa;

++*var1;                        // ++*pa;

*var3 = *var3 * *var1;          // *pb = *pb * pa;
```

And we get the following code after renaming and rearranging:

```
int a, b;
int *pa, *pb;

pa = &a;
pb = &b;

*pa = 1;
*pb = 1;

*pb = *pb + *pa;

++*pa;

*pb = *pb * *pa;
```

If we look at the project source code PointersAsVariables.cpp, we see the same code compiled into the executable file that we were disassembling.

Example of Disassembly Output: Optimized Program

The optimized program (compiled with -O2) contains fewer CPU instructions:

```
(gdb) disass main
Dump of assembler code for function main:
   0x0000000000400450 <+0>:      adrp    x1, 0x420000
```

```
0x0000000000400454 <+4>:      add     x0, x1, #0x28
0x0000000000400458 <+8>:      add     x3, x0, #0x8
0x000000000040045c <+12>:     str     x3, [x1,#40]
0x0000000000400460 <+16>:     mov     w1, #0x2          // #2
0x0000000000400464 <+20>:     add     x2, x0, #0x18
0x0000000000400468 <+24>:     str     w1, [x0,#8]
0x000000000040046c <+28>:     mov     w1, #0x4          // #4
0x0000000000400470 <+32>:     str     x2, [x0,#16]
0x0000000000400474 <+36>:     str     w1, [x0,#24]
0x0000000000400478 <+40>:     mov     w0, #0x0          // #0
0x000000000040047c <+44>:     ret
End of assembler dump.
```

In this code, we also see instructions in the format str regSrc, [regDst, #offset]. It means that the offset value is added to the address in the regDst register. The value from the regSrc register is moved to the memory cell pointed by the combined address regDst + offset:

```
[regDst + offset] <- regSrc
```

We see that the compiler was able to figure out the result of computation: a = 2; b = 4. However, one question remains: Why did the compiler not optimize away instructions initializing **pa** and **pb** variables? The answer lies in the nature of a separate compilation model in C and C++. We can compile several compilation unit (.c or .cpp) files separately and independently. Therefore, there is no guarantee that another compilation unit would not reference our globally declared and defined **pa** and **pb** variables.

Summary

In this chapter, we used our assembly language knowledge to reconstruct C and C++ code that uses pointers. We also compared the disassembly of the optimized code.

The next chapter looks at the stack memory layout and its operations, branch instructions, and function calls. We also explore a call stack using the GDB debugger.

CHAPTER 9

Memory and Stacks

Stack: A Definition

A stack is a simple computational device with two operations, push and pop, that allows us to pile up data to remember it in LIFO (Last In First Out) manner and quickly retrieve the last piled data item as shown in Figure 9-1.

© Dmitry Vostokov 2023
D. Vostokov, *Foundations of ARM64 Linux Debugging, Disassembling, and Reversing*,
https://doi.org/10.1007/978-1-4842-9082-8_9

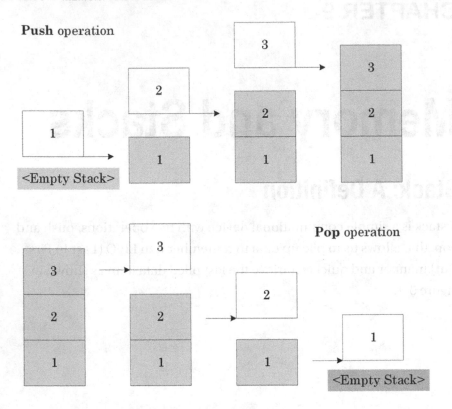

Figure 9-1. *Stack operations illustrated*

Stack Implementation in Memory

The CPU SP register (Stack Pointer) points to the top of a stack. As shown in Figure 9-2, a stack grows toward lower memory addresses with every push operation, and this is implemented as the SP register decrements by 16 (the ARM64 stack address must be aligned by 16 bytes), then moving a value or a pair of values using STR or STP instructions with the so-called preindexing. We can read the top stack value using the following instruction:

```
ldr  x0, [sp]
```

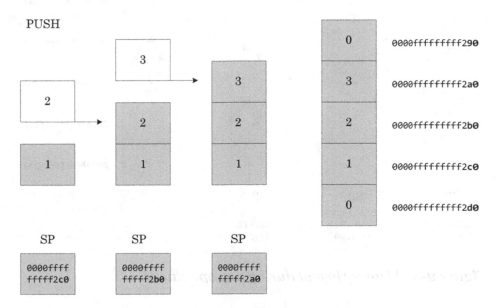

Figure 9-2. *Memory layout during push operations*

The opposite pop operation increments the value of the SP register, as shown in Figure 9-3.

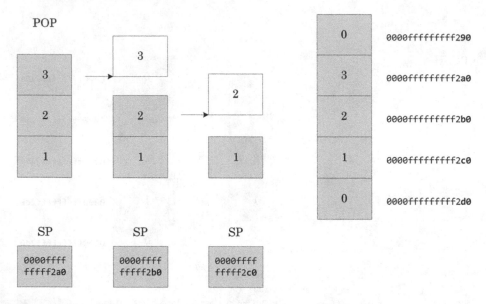

Figure 9-3. *Memory layout during pop operations*

Things to Remember

Here is the summary of what we have learned about stacks with the last three points covered in the subsequent chapters of this book:

- Stack operations are LIFO – Last In First Out.

- The stack grows down in memory.

- The SP register points to the top of a stack.

- SP must be aligned by 16 bytes.

- Stacks are used for storing a return address for the BL instruction.

- Stacks are used for passing additional parameters to functions.

- Stacks are used for storing function parameter values and local and temporary variables.

Stack Push Implementation

Push is implemented via these instructions:

```
str  x0, [sp, #-16]!          // sp <- sp - 16
                              // [sp] <- x0

stp  x0, x1, [sp, #-16]!      // sp <- sp - 16
                              // [sp] <- x0
                              // [sp+8] <- x1
```

Stack Pop Implementation

Pop is implemented via these instructions:

```
ldr  x0, [sp], #16            // x0 <- [sp]
                              // sp <- sp + 16

ldp  x0, x1, [sp] #16         // x0 <- [sp]
                              // x1 <- [sp+8]
                              // sp <- sp + 16
```

Register Review

So far, we have seen and used general-purpose CPU registers:

- X0/W0

- X1/W1

- X2/W2

- X3/W3

- X4/W4

- ...

- X30/W30

We also have special-purpose registers:

- XZR/WZR (Zero Register)

- PC (Instruction Pointer)

- SP (Stack Pointer)

Application Memory Simplified

When an executable file is loaded into memory, its header and sections are mapped to memory pages. Some data and code are copied unmodified, but some data is initialized and expanded. The first stack is also created at this stage. The PC register is set to point to the first program instruction, and SP points to the top of the stack. This simplified process is shown in Figure 9-4.

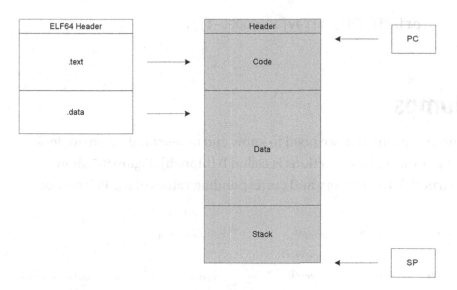

Figure 9-4. *Application memory layout*

Stack Overflow

By default, the stack size is limited (system and limit dependent, and it is 8192Kb or 8388608 bytes) on our system. If a stack grows beyond the reserved limit, a stack overflow occurs (segmentation fault). It can be caused by an unlimited recursion, deep recursion, or very large local variables:

```
int func()
{
    func();
    return 0;
}
int func2()
{
    int array[10000000] = { 1 };
```

```
    printf("%d", array[10000000-1]);
}
```

Jumps

Another instruction we need to know and understand before we look deeper into C/C++ functions is called B (branch). Figure 9-5 shows instructions in memory and corresponding values of the PC register.

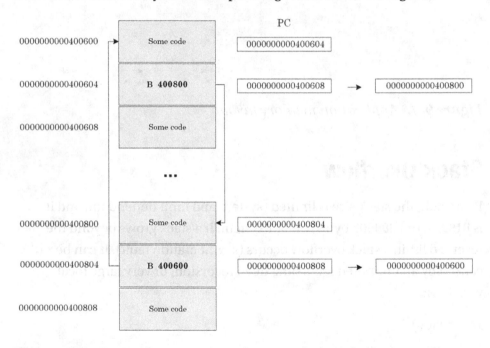

Figure 9-5. *Example memory and register layout for B instruction execution*

We see that the B instruction changes PC to point to another memory address, and the program execution continues from that location. The code shown in Figure 9-5 loops indefinitely: this can be considered a hang and CPU spike.

There is also a BR indirect branch instruction to the address located in a register. It is illustrated in Figure 9-6.

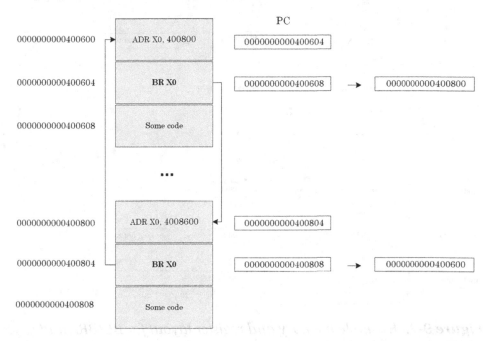

Figure 9-6. *Example memory and register layout for BR instruction execution*

Calls

We discuss two essential instructions that make the implementation of C and C++ function calls. They are called BL/BRL and RET. The return address is saved in the so-called Link Register (LR, X30). Figure 9-7 shows instructions in memory and corresponding values of PC and LR registers.

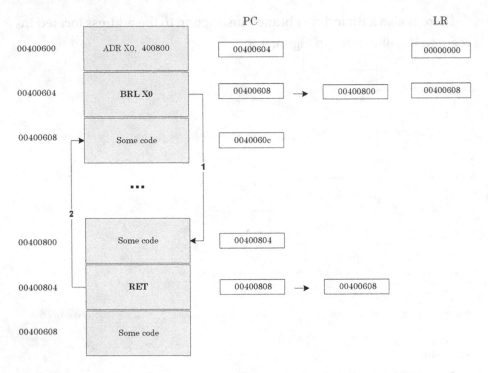

Figure 9-7. *Example memory and register layout for BL/BRL and RET instruction execution*

We see that the BRL instruction saves the current value of PC to LR and changes PC to point to another memory address. Then the program execution continues from the new location. The RET instruction restores the saved PC value from LR to the PC register. Then the program execution resumes at the memory location after the BRL instruction. If you need nested calls, you need to save the current LR on the stack manually.

Call Stack

If one function (the caller) calls another function (the callee) in C and C++, the resulting code is implemented using BL/BRL instructions, and during its execution, the return address is saved in LR. If the callee calls another

116

function, the previous LR value would be lost, so it is saved on the stack, and so on. Therefore, we have the so-called call stack of return addresses. Let us see this with a simple but trimmed-down example.

Suppose we have three functions with their code occupying the following addresses:

```
func  0000000140001000 - 0000000140001100
func2 0000000140001101 - 0000000140001200
func3 0000000140001201 - 0000000140001300
```

We also have the following code where *func* calls *func2*, and *func2* calls *func3*:

```
void func()
{
    func2();
}
void func2()
{
    func3();
}
```

When *func* calls *func2*, the caller's return address is saved on the stack, and SP points to some value in the 0000000140001000–0000000140001100 range, say 0000000140001020. When *func2* calls *func3*, the caller's return address is also saved on the stack, and SP points to some value in the 0000000140001101–0000000140001200 range, say 0000000140001180. If we interrupt *func3* with a debugger and inspect the PC register, we would find its value in the range of 0000000140001201–0000000140001300, say 0000000140001250. Therefore, we have the idealized memory and register layout shown in Figure 9-8 (the usual function prolog is not shown; we will learn about it in the next chapter).

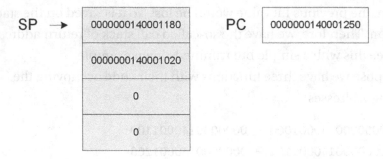

Figure 9-8. *Example memory and register layout for call stack*

The debugger examines the value of the PC register and the values on top of the stack and then reconstructs this call stack:

```
func3
func2
func
```

The debugger gets address ranges corresponding to *func*, *func2*, and *func3* from the so-called symbolic information, which may be either stored inside an executable file or in some external file that needs to be referenced explicitly.

Exploring Stack in GDB

To see the call stack in real action, we have a project called "SimpleStack," and it can be downloaded from

github.com/apress/arm64-linux-debugging-disassembling-reversing/Chapter9/

We compile the files and load the executable into GDB:

```
$ gcc SimpleStack.c func.c func2.c func3.c -o SimpleStack
```

```
$ gdb ./SimpleStack
GNU gdb (GDB) Red Hat Enterprise Linux 7.6.1-120.0.2.el7
Copyright (C) 2013 Free Software Foundation, Inc.
License GPLv3+: GNU GPL version 3 or later <http://gnu.org/
licenses/gpl.html>
This is free software: you are free to change and
redistribute it.
There is NO WARRANTY, to the extent permitted by law.  Type
"show copying"
and "show warranty" for details.
This GDB was configured as "aarch64-redhat-linux-gnu".
For bug reporting instructions, please see:
<http://www.gnu.org/software/gdb/bugs/>...
Reading symbols from /home/coredump/pflddr/A64/Chapter9/
SimpleStack...(no debugging symbols found)...done.
```

Then we put a breakpoint on the *main* function and run the program until GDB breaks in:

```
(gdb) break main
Breakpoint 1 at 0x4005c0

(gdb) run
Starting program: /home/coredump/pflddr/A64/Chapter9/./
SimpleStack

Breakpoint 1, 0x00000000004005c0 in main ()
Missing separate debuginfos, use: debuginfo-install
glibc-2.17-325.0.2.el7_9.aarch64
```

The function *func3* has a breakpoint instruction inside that allows a debugger to break in and stop the program execution to inspect its state. We resume our program execution from our breakpoint in the *main* function to allow the *main* function to call *func*, *func* to call *func2*, *func2* to call *func3*, and inside *func3* to execute the explicit breakpoint:

```
(gdb) continue
Continuing.

Program received signal SIGTRAP, Trace/breakpoint trap.
0x0000000000400600 in func3 ()

(gdb) info registers $pc $sp
pc                  0x400600  4195840
sp                  0xfffffffff290   281474976707216

(gdb) x/i $pc
=> 0x400600 <func3>:     brk     #0x3
```

Now we can inspect the top of the stack:

```
(gdb) x/10g $sp
0xfffffffff290: 0x0000fffffffff2a0      0x00000000004005e4
0xfffffffff2a0: 0x0000fffffffff2b0      0x00000000004005cc
0xfffffffff2b0: 0x0000fffffffff2d0      0x0000fffff7e22668
0xfffffffff2c0: 0x0000fffffffff418      0x0000000100000000
0xfffffffff2d0: 0x0000000000000000      0x000000000040049c
```

The data is meaningless for us, and we use another command variant to dump memory with corresponding symbols:

```
(gdb) x/10a $sp
0xfffffffff290: 0xfffffffff2a0  0x4005e4 <func+12>
0xfffffffff2a0: 0xfffffffff2b0  0x4005cc <main+20>
0xfffffffff2b0: 0xfffffffff2d0  0xfffff7e22668 <__libc_start_
main+236>
0xfffffffff2c0: 0xfffffffff418  0x100000000
0xfffffffff2d0: 0x0     0x40049c <_start+76>
```

The current value of PC points to *func3*, and return addresses on the stack are shown in bold. GDB is able to reconstruct the following call stack, stack trace, or backtrace (bt):

```
(gdb) set backtrace past-main on

(gdb) bt
#0  0x0000000000400600 in func3 ()
#1  0x00000000004005f8 in func2 ()
#2  0x00000000004005e4 in func ()
#3  0x00000000004005cc in main ()
#4  0x0000ffffff7e22668 in __libc_start_main () from /lib64/
libc.so.6
#5  0x000000000040049c in _start ()
```

We don't see the *func2* return address on the stack, but we can get it from the current value of the LR register:

```
(gdb) x/a $lr
0x4005f8 <func2+12>:     0xd65f03c0a8c17bfd
```

Summary

In this chapter, we looked at the stack memory layout and stack operations, branch and branch and link instructions, and function call memory layout. We also explored a call stack using the GDB debugger commands.

In the next chapter, we look into further details of the stack layout of the more complex code, for example, arrays, local variables, function prolog, and epilog. Finally, we disassemble and analyze code that uses local variables.

CHAPTER 10

Frame Pointer and Local Variables

Stack Usage

In addition to storage for return addresses, a stack is used to pass additional parameters to functions (if you have more than eight parameters) and store local variables. The stack is also used to save and restore values held in registers when we want to preserve them during some computation or across function calls. For example, suppose we want to call some function, but at the same time, we have valuable data in registers X0 and X1. The function code may overwrite X0 and X1 values, so we temporarily save their current values on the stack:

```
mov   x0, #10
mov   x1, #20
...
...
...                        // now we want to preserve
                              X0 and X1
stp   x0, x1, [sp, #-16]!  // store the pair at once
bl    func
ldp   x0, x1, [sp], #16    // restore the pair at once
```

© Dmitry Vostokov 2023

D. Vostokov, *Foundations of ARM64 Linux Debugging, Disassembling, and Reversing*,
https://doi.org/10.1007/978-1-4842-9082-8_10

Register Review

So far, we have encountered these registers:

- X0/W0 (among its specific uses are to contain function return values)

- X1/W1–X29/W29

- XZR/WZR (X31, zero register)

- LR (X30, Link Register, stores the return address)

- PC (Instruction Pointer, points to the next instruction to be executed)

- SP (Stack Pointer, points to the top of the stack)

We come to the next important register on Linux platforms called Base Pointer register or sometimes as Stack Frame Pointer register. It is X29, and it is used for stack reconstruction.

Addressing Array Elements

We can also consider stack memory as an array of memory cells, and any general-purpose register can be used to address stack memory elements in the way shown in Figure 10-1, where it slides into the frame of stack memory called a stack frame. The first diagram depicts 64-bit (doubleword) memory cells, and the second depicts 32-bit (word) memory cells. Offsets for addresses are in hexadecimal, but for accessing values, offsets are in decimal, like we usually see in GDB disassembly.

	Address of the element	Value of the element
0	0010001000 X0-0x20	[X0, -#32]
0	0010001008 X0-0x18	[X0, -#24]
0	0010001010 X0-0x10	[X0, -#16]
0	0010001018 X0-0x08	[X0, -#8]
X0 → 0	0010001020 X0	[X0]
0	0010001028 X0+0x08	[X0, #8]
0	0010001030 X0+0x10	[X0, #16]
0	0010001038 X0+0x18	[X0, #24]

	Address	Value	
0	0010001018	X0-0x08	[X0, -#8]
0	001000101C	X0-0x04	[X0, -#4]
X0 → 0	0010001020	X0	[X0]
0	0010001024	X0+0x04	[X0, #4]
0	0010001028	X0+0x08	[X0, #8]
0	001000102C	X0+0x0C	[X0, #12]

Figure 10-1. *Example memory layout when addressing array elements*

Stack Structure (No Function Parameters)

Suppose the following function is called:

```
void func()
{
    int var1, var2;
    // body code
    // ...
}
```

Before the function body code is executed, the following pointers are set up:

- [SP, #8] contains local variable var1 (word).

- [SP, #12] contains local variable var2 (word).

It is illustrated in Figure 10-2. Stack room space needs to be aligned by 16 bytes by ARM64 specification.

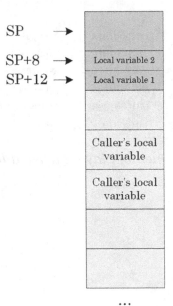

Figure 10-2. *Stack memory layout without function parameters*

Function Prolog

The sequence of instructions resulting in the initialization of the SP register, saving X29/LR (if there are further calls inside), and making room for local variables is called the function prolog. One example of it is Figure 10-3, where *func* calls *func2*, which has one local variable var. Sometimes, saving necessary registers is also considered as part of a function prolog.

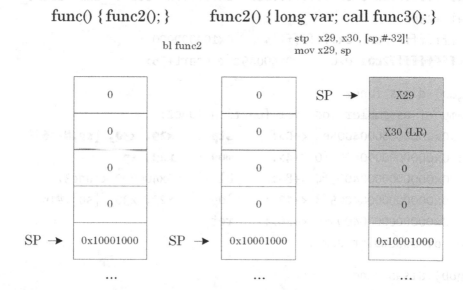

Figure 10-3. *Example memory layout for function prolog*

Raw Stack (No Local Variables and Function Parameters)

Now we can understand additional data that appear on the raw stack together with function return addresses that we saw in Chapter 9 project "SimpleStack":

```
(gdb) info registers $sp $x29 $lr
sp              0xfffffffff280    281474976707200
x29             0xfffffffff280    281474976707200
lr              0x4005f8 4195832
```

```
(gdb) x/10a $sp
0xfffffffff280: 0xfffffffff290    0x4005e4 <func+12>
0xfffffffff290: 0xfffffffff2a0    0x4005cc <main+20>
0xfffffffff2a0: 0xfffffffff2c0    0xffff7e22668 <__libc_start_
main+236>
0xfffffffff2b0: 0xfffffffff408    0x100000000
0xfffffffff2c0: 0x0        0x40049c <_start+76>
```

```
(gdb) disas func2
Dump of assembler code for function func2:
    0x00000000004005ec <+0>:     stp     x29, x30, [sp,#-16]!
    0x00000000004005f0 <+4>:     mov     x29, sp
    0x00000000004005f4 <+8>:     bl      0x400600 <func3>
    0x00000000004005f8 <+12>:    ldp     x29, x30, [sp],#16
    0x00000000004005fc <+16>:    ret
End of assembler dump.
```

```
(gdb) disas func
Dump of assembler code for function func:
    0x00000000004005d8 <+0>:     stp     x29, x30, [sp,#-16]!
    0x00000000004005dc <+4>:     mov     x29, sp
    0x00000000004005e0 <+8>:     bl      0x4005ec <func2>
    0x00000000004005e4 <+12>:    ldp     x29, x30, [sp],#16
    0x00000000004005e8 <+16>:    ret
End of assembler dump.
```

```
(gdb) disas main
Dump of assembler code for function main:
```

```
0x00000000004005b8 <+0>:    stp    x29, x30, [sp,#-32]!
0x00000000004005bc <+4>:    mov    x29, sp
0x00000000004005c0 <+8>:    str    w0, [x29,#28]
0x00000000004005c4 <+12>:   str    x1, [x29,#16]
0x00000000004005c8 <+16>:   bl     0x4005d8 <func>
0x00000000004005cc <+20>:   mov    w0, #0x0                // #0
0x00000000004005d0 <+24>:   ldp    x29, x30, [sp],#32
0x00000000004005d4 <+28>:   ret
```

Function Epilog

Before the function code returns to the caller, it must restore the previous values of X29 and X30 (LR) registers to allow the caller to resume its execution from the correct address, previously saved in LR, and continue addressing its own stack frame properly. This sequence of instructions is called the function epilog, and it is shown in Figure 10-4.

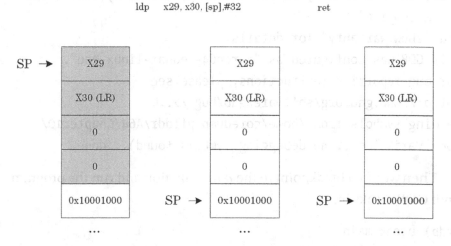

Figure 10-4. Example memory layout for function epilog

"Local Variables" Project

The project for this chapter can be downloaded from

github.com/apress/arm64-linux-debugging-disassembling-
reversing/Chapter10/

We compile the file and load the executable into GDB:

```
$ gcc LocalVariables.cpp -o LocalVariables


$ gdb ./LocalVariables
GNU gdb (GDB) Red Hat Enterprise Linux 7.6.1-120.0.2.el7
Copyright (C) 2013 Free Software Foundation, Inc.
License GPLv3+: GNU GPL version 3 or later <http://gnu.org/
licenses/gpl.html>
This is free software: you are free to change and
redistribute it.
There is NO WARRANTY, to the extent permitted by law.  Type
"show copying"
and "show warranty" for details.
This GDB was configured as "aarch64-redhat-linux-gnu".
For bug reporting instructions, please see:
<http://www.gnu.org/software/gdb/bugs/>...
Reading symbols from /home/coredump/pflddr/A64/Chapter10/
LocalVariables...(no debugging symbols found)...done.
```

Then we put a breakpoint to the *main* function and run the program until GDB breaks in:

```
(gdb) break main
Breakpoint 1 at 0x4005c0

(gdb) run
```

Starting program: /home/coredump/pflddr/A64/Chapter10/./
LocalVariables

Breakpoint 1, 0x00000000004005c0 in main ()
Missing separate debuginfos, use: debuginfo-install
glibc-2.17-325.0.2.el7_9.aarch64

Next, we disassemble our *main* function:

```
(gdb) disas main
Dump of assembler code for function main:
   0x00000000004005b8 <+0>:     sub     sp, sp, #0x10
   0x00000000004005bc <+4>:     mov     w0, #0x1        // #1
=> 0x00000000004005c0 <+8>:     str     w0, [sp,#12]
   0x00000000004005c4 <+12>:    mov     w0, #0x1        // #1
   0x00000000004005c8 <+16>:    str     w0, [sp,#8]
   0x00000000004005cc <+20>:    ldr     w1, [sp,#8]
   0x00000000004005d0 <+24>:    ldr     w0, [sp,#12]
   0x00000000004005d4 <+28>:    add     w0, w1, w0
   0x00000000004005d8 <+32>:    str     w0, [sp,#8]
   0x00000000004005dc <+36>:    ldr     w0, [sp,#12]
   0x00000000004005e0 <+40>:    add     w0, w0, #0x1
   0x00000000004005e4 <+44>:    str     w0, [sp,#12]
   0x00000000004005e8 <+48>:    ldr     w1, [sp,#8]
   0x00000000004005ec <+52>:    ldr     w0, [sp,#12]
   0x00000000004005f0 <+56>:    mul     w0, w1, w0
   0x00000000004005f4 <+60>:    str     w0, [sp,#8]
   0x00000000004005f8 <+64>:    mov     w0, #0x0        // #0
   0x00000000004005fc <+68>:    add     sp, sp, #0x10
   0x0000000000400600 <+72>:    ret
End of assembler dump.
```

Its source code is the following:

```
int main()
{
    int a, b;

a = 1;
    b = 1;

b = b + a;
    ++a;
    b = b * a;

return 0;
}
```

The following is the same assembly language code but with comments showing operations in pseudo-code and highlighting the function prolog and epilog:

```
    0x00000000004005b8 <+0>:      sub      sp, sp, #0x10
// establishing stack frame
    0x00000000004005bc <+4>:      mov      w0,
#0x1      // w0 <- 1
=> 0x00000000004005c0 <+8>:      str      w0, [sp,#12]
// [a] <- w0
    0x00000000004005c4 <+12>:     mov      w0,
#0x1      // w0 <- 1
    0x00000000004005c8 <+16>:     str      w0, [sp,#8]
// [b] <- w0
    0x00000000004005cc <+20>:     ldr      w1, [sp,#8]
// w1 <- [b]
```

```
   0x00000000004005d0 <+24>:    ldr     w0, [sp,#12]
// w0 <- [a]
   0x00000000004005d4 <+28>:    add     w0, w1, w0
// w0 <- w1 + w0
   0x00000000004005d8 <+32>:    str     w0, [sp,#8]
// [b] <- w0
   0x00000000004005dc <+36>:    ldr     w0, [sp,#12]
// w0 <- [a]
   0x00000000004005e0 <+40>:    add     w0, w0, #0x1
// w0 <- w0 + 1
   0x00000000004005e4 <+44>:    str     w0, [sp,#12]
// [a] <- w0
   0x00000000004005e8 <+48>:    ldr     w1, [sp,#8]
// w1 <- [b]
   0x00000000004005ec <+52>:    ldr     w0, [sp,#12]
// w0 <- [a]
   0x00000000004005f0 <+56>:    mul     w0, w1, w0
// w0 <- w1 * w0
   0x00000000004005f4 <+60>:    str     w0, [sp,#8]
// [b] <- w0
   0x00000000004005f8 <+64>:    mov     w0, #0x0
// w0 <- 0 (return value)
   0x00000000004005fc <+68>:    add     sp, sp, #0x10
// restoring previous frame
   0x0000000000400600 <+72>:    ret
// return
```

Disassembly of Optimized Executable

If we compile LocalVariables.cpp with the -O1 option, we see a very simple code that just returns zero:

```
(gdb) disas main
Dump of assembler code for function main:
   0x00000000004005b8 <+0>:        mov      w0, #0x0                     // #0
   0x00000000004005bc <+4>:        ret
End of assembler dump.
```

Where is all the code we have seen in the previous version? It was optimized away by the compiler because the results of our calculation are never used. Variables **a** and **b** are local to the *main* function, and their values are not accessible outside when we return from the function.

Summary

In this chapter, we looked into the stack layout of the more complex code: addressing arrays, local variables, and compiler-emitted code for the function prolog and epilog. Finally, we disassembled and analyzed code that used local variables and compared it to the optimized version.

The next chapter looks at function parameters and their stack layout. Finally, we disassemble and analyze another project with function parameters and local variables.

CHAPTER 11

Function Parameters

"FunctionParameters" Project

This chapter teaches how a caller function passes its parameters via registers and how a callee (the called function) accesses them. We use the following project that can be downloaded from this link:

github.com/apress/arm64-linux-debugging-disassembling-reversing/Chapter11/

Here is the project source code:

```
// FunctionParameters.cpp
int arithmetic (int a, int b);

int main(int argc, char* argv[])
{
    int result = arithmetic (1, 1);

return 0;
}

// Arithmetic.cpp
int arithmetic (int a, int b)
{
    b = b + a;
    ++a;
```

© Dmitry Vostokov 2023
D. Vostokov, *Foundations of ARM64 Linux Debugging, Disassembling, and Reversing*,
https://doi.org/10.1007/978-1-4842-9082-8_11

```
    b = b * a;

    return b;
}
```

Stack Structure

Recall from the previous chapter that X0–X29 registers are used to address stack memory locations. It was illustrated in Figure 10-1 for X0. Here, we provide a typical example of the stack memory layout for the following function where the X29 register is used:

```
void func(int Param1, int Param2)
{
    int var1, var2;
    // stack memory layout at this point, X29 = SP
    // [X29]       = previous X29
    // [x29, #8]   = LR
    // [x29, #24]  = Saved Param2 (word)
    // [x29, #28]  = Saved Param1 (word)
    // [x29, #40]  = var2 (word)
    // [x29, #44]  = var1 (word)
    // ...
}
```

The typical stack frame memory layout for the function with two arguments and two local variables is illustrated in Figure 11-1.

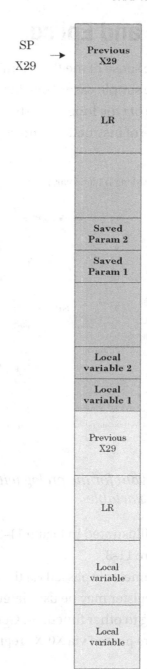

SP
X29

Previous X29

LR

Saved Param 2

Saved Param 1

Local variable 2

Local variable 1

Previous X29

LR

Local variable

Local variable

Figure 11-1. *Stack memory layout for the function with two arguments and two local variables*

Function Prolog and Epilog

Now, before we try to make sense of the FunctionParameters project disassembly, we look at the simple case of one function parameter of type long and one local variable of type long to illustrate the standard function prolog and epilog sequence of instructions and corresponding stack memory changes.

func() { func2(1); }   func2(long i) { long var; }

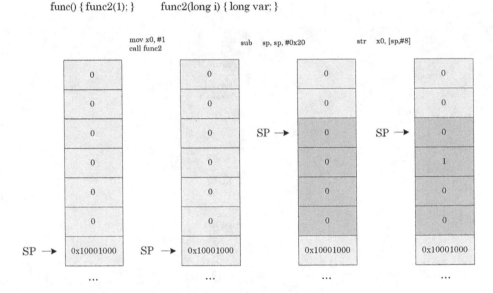

Figure 11-2. *Memory layout for the prolog with one function parameter and one local variable*

The function prolog is illustrated in Figure 11-2, and the function epilog is illustrated in Figure 11-3.

Here, the function parameter is passed via the X0 register. It is saved on the stack because the register may be used later in calculations or the function parameter passing to other functions. Generally, the first eight parameters of a function are passed via X0–X7 registers from left to the right when parameters are doublewords like pointers or long values and via W0–W7 registers when parameters are words like integers. Additional parameters are passed via the stack locations using STR/STP instructions.

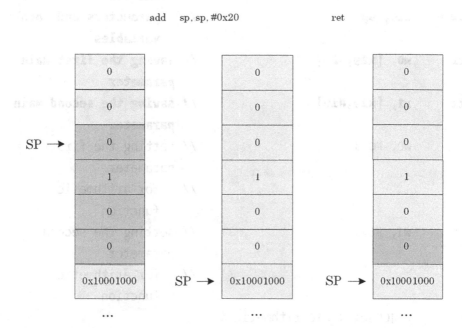

Figure 11-3. *Memory layout for the epilog with one function parameter and one local variable*

We also see that local variables are not initialized by default when their storage space is allocated via the SUB instruction and not cleared during the epilog. Whatever memory contents were there before allocation, it becomes the local variable values, the so-called garbage values.

Project Disassembled Code with Comments

Here is a commented code disassembly of *main* and *arithmetic* with memory addresses removed for visual clarity:

```
main:

stp     x29, x30, [sp,#-48]!      // establishing stack
                                     frame for

mov     x29, sp                  //   parameters and local
                                     variables

str     w0, [x29,#28]            // saving the first main
                                     parameter

str     x1, [x29,#16]            // saving the second main
                                     parameter

mov     w0, #0x1                 // setting the first
                                     parameter
                                 //   for arithmetic
                                     function

mov     w1, #0x1                 // setting the second
                                     parameter
                                 //   for arithmetic
                                     function

bl      0x4005e4 <_Z10arithmeticii>
str     w0, [x29,#44]            // setting the result
                                     local variab;e

mov     w0, #0x0                 // main should return 0
ldp     x29, x30, [sp],#48       // restoring the previous
                                     stack frame,
                                 //   frame and link
                                     registers

ret                              // return from main

arithmetic:

sub     sp, sp, #0x10            // establishing stack
                                     frame for
```

```
                                   //    parameters and local
                                   //    variables
str     w0, [sp,#12]               // saving the first
                                   // arithmetic parameter (a)
str     w1, [sp,#8]                // saving the second
                                   // arithmetic parameter (b)
ldr     w1, [sp,#8]               // w1 <- [b]
ldr     w0, [sp,#12]              // w0 <- [a]
add     w0, w1, w0                // w0 <- w1 + w0
str     w0, [sp,#8]               // [b] <- w0
ldr     w0, [sp,#12]              // w0 <- [a]
add     w0, w0, #0x1              // w0 <- w0 + 1
str     w0, [sp,#12]              // [a] <- w0
ldr     w1, [sp,#8]               // w1 <- [b]
ldr     w0, [sp,#12]              // w0 <- [a]
mul     w0, w1, w0                // w0 <- w1 * w0
str     w0, [sp,#8]               // [b] <- w0
ldr     w0, [sp,#8]               // w0 <- [b]
                                   //    return result
add     sp, sp, #0x10             // restoring the previous
                                   // stack frame
ret                                // return from arithmetic
```

We can put a breakpoint on the first arithmetic calculation address and examine raw stack data pointed to by the SP register:

```
$ gcc FunctionParameters.cpp Arithmetic.cpp -o
FunctionParameters

$ gdb ./FunctionParameters
GNU gdb (GDB) Red Hat Enterprise Linux 7.6.1-120.0.2.el7
Copyright (C) 2013 Free Software Foundation, Inc.
```

License GPLv3+: GNU GPL version 3 or later <http://gnu.org/
licenses/gpl.html>
This is free software: you are free to change and
redistribute it.
There is NO WARRANTY, to the extent permitted by law. Type
"show copying"
and "show warranty" for details.
This GDB was configured as "aarch64-redhat-linux-gnu".
For bug reporting instructions, please see:
<http://www.gnu.org/software/gdb/bugs/>...
Reading symbols from /home/coredump/pflddr/A64/Chapter11/
FunctionParameters...(no debugging symbols found)...done.

(gdb) break main
Breakpoint 1 at 0x4005c0

(gdb) run
Starting program: /home/coredump/pflddr/A64/Chapter11/./
FunctionParameters

Breakpoint 1, 0x00000000004005c0 in main ()
Missing separate debuginfos, use: debuginfo-install
glibc-2.17-325.0.2.el7_9.aarch64

(gdb) disas arithmetic
Dump of assembler code for function _Z10arithmeticii:
```
   0x00000000004005e4 <+0>:     sub     sp, sp, #0x10
   0x00000000004005e8 <+4>:     str     w0, [sp,#12]
   0x00000000004005ec <+8>:     str     w1, [sp,#8]
   0x00000000004005f0 <+12>:    ldr     w1, [sp,#8]
   0x00000000004005f4 <+16>:    ldr     w0, [sp,#12]
   0x00000000004005f8 <+20>:    add     w0, w1, w0
   0x00000000004005fc <+24>:    str     w0, [sp,#8]
```

```
0x0000000000400600 <+28>:      ldr    w0, [sp,#12]
0x0000000000400604 <+32>:      add    w0, w0, #0x1
0x0000000000400608 <+36>:      str    w0, [sp,#12]
0x000000000040060c <+40>:      ldr    w1, [sp,#8]
0x0000000000400610 <+44>:      ldr    w0, [sp,#12]
0x0000000000400614 <+48>:      mul    w0, w1, w0
0x0000000000400618 <+52>:      str    w0, [sp,#8]
0x000000000040061c <+56>:      ldr    w0, [sp,#8]
0x0000000000400620 <+60>:      add    sp, sp, #0x10
0x0000000000400624 <+64>:      ret
End of assembler dump.

(gdb) break *0x00000000004005f0
Breakpoint 2 at 0x4005f0

(gdb) continue
Continuing.

Breakpoint 2, 0x00000000004005f0 in arithmetic(int, int) ()

(gdb) info registers $sp
sp            0xfffffffff270    281474976707184

(gdb) x/a $lr
0x4005d4 <main+28>:        0x52800000b9002fa0

(gdb) x/10a $sp-0x20
0xfffffffff250: 0xfffff7fcee54 <_dl_fini>          0x400628 <__
libc_csu_init>
0xfffffffff260: 0xfffffffff270  0x400680 <__libc_csu_init+88>
0xfffffffff270: 0xfffffffff2b0  0x100000001    // (b, a)
0xfffffffff280: 0xfffffffff2b0  0xfffff7e22668 <__libc_start_
main+236>
0xfffffffff290: 0xfffffffff3f8  0x1f7e22628
```

```
(gdb) x/20x $sp-0x20
0xfffffffff250:
0xf7fcee54      0x0000ffff      0x00400628      0x00000000
0xfffffffff260:
0xffff270       0x0000ffff      0x00400680      0x00000000
0xfffffffff270:
0xffff2b0       0x0000ffff      0x00000001      0x00000001
0xfffffffff280:
0xffff2b0       0x0000ffff      0xf7e22668      0x0000ffff
0xfffffffff290:
0xffff3f8       0x0000ffff      0xf7e22628      0x00000001
```

Parameter Mismatch Problem

Consider this typical ABI (Application Binary Interface) mismatch problem. The function *main* calls *func* with two parameters:

```
// main.c
int main ()
{
    long locVar;
    func (1, 2);
    return 0;
}
```

The caller passes 1 in X0 and 2 in X1. However, the callee expects three parameters instead of two:

```
// func.c
int func (int a, int b, int c)
```

```
{
    // code to use parameters
    return 0;
}
```

We see that the parameter on the raw stack gets its value from some random value in X2 that was never set by the caller. It is clearly a software defect (bug).

Summary

This chapter looked at function parameters and their stack layout. We disassembled and analyzed the stack structure of the project with function parameters and local variables. Finally, we looked at a parameter mismatch problem.

The next chapter is about CPU state flags, comparison instructions, conditional branches, and function return values.

CHAPTER 12

More Instructions

PSTATE Flags

In addition to registers, the CPU also contains a 32-bit PSTATE where four individual bits N, Z, C, and V (Figure 12-1) are set or cleared in response to arithmetic and other operations. Separate machine instructions can manipulate some bit values, and their values affect code execution.

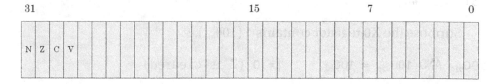

Figure 12-1. *PSTATE flags*

These flags have their own special register NZCV.

Testing for 0

The Z bit in the NZCV register is set to one if the instruction result is zero and cleared otherwise. This bit is affected by

- Arithmetic instructions with the S suffix (e.g., ADDS, SUBS, MULS)

© Dmitry Vostokov 2023
D. Vostokov, *Foundations of ARM64 Linux Debugging, Disassembling, and Reversing*,
https://doi.org/10.1007/978-1-4842-9082-8_12

- Logical compare instruction (TST)

- "Arithmetical" compare instruction (CMP)

TST – Logical Compare

This instruction computes bitwise logical AND between both operands and sets flags (including Z) according to the computed result (which is discarded):

```
TST  reg, reg
TST  reg, #imm
```

Examples:

```
TST  X0, #4
```

Suppose the X0 register contains 4 (100_{bin}):

```
100bin AND 100bin = 100bin      != 0 (Z is cleared)
```

```
TST  W1, #1
```

Suppose W1 contains 0 (0_{bin}):

```
0bin AND 1bin = 0bin      == 0 (Z is set)
```

Here is the TST instruction in pseudo-code (details not relevant to the Z bit are omitted):

```
TEMP <- OPERAND1 AND OPERAND2
IF TEMP = 0 THEN
      Z <- 1
ELSE
      Z <- 0
```

CMP – Compare Two Operands

This instruction compares the first operand with the second and sets flags (including Z) according to the computed result (which is discarded). The comparison is performed by subtracting the second operand from the first (like the SUBS instruction: sub xzr, x1, #4).

```
CMP   reg, reg
CMP   reg, #imm
```

Examples:

```
CMP   X1, #0
```

Suppose X1 contains 0:

```
0 - 0   == 0 (Z is set)
```

```
CMP   W0, #0x16
```

Suppose W0 contains 4_{hex}:

$4_{hex} - 16_{hex}$ $= FFFFFFEE_{hex}$!= 0 (Z is cleared)
$4_{dec} - 22_{dec}$ $= -18_{dec}$

Here is the CMP instruction in pseudo-code (details not relevant to the Z bit are omitted):

```
TEMP <- OPERAND1 - OPERAND2
IF TEMP = 0 THEN
     Z <- 1
ELSE
     Z <- 0
```

TST or CMP?

Both instructions are equivalent if we want to test for zero, but the CMP instruction affects more flags than TST:

```
TST   X0, X0
CMP   X0, #0
```

The CMP instruction is used to compare for inequality (the TST instruction cannot be used here):

```
CMP   X0, #0      // > 0 or < 0 ?
```

The TST instruction is used to see if individual bits are set:

```
TST   X0, #2      // 2 == 0010bin  or in C language: if
(var & 0x2)
```

Examples where X0 has the value of 2:

```
TST   X0, #4    # 0010bin AND 0100bin = 0000bin (ZF is set)
TST   X0, #6    # 0010bin AND 0110bin = 0010bin (Z is cleared)
```

Conditional Jumps

Consider these two C or C++ code fragments:

```
if (a == 0)                    if (a != 0)
{                              {
    ++a;                           ++a;
}                              }
else                           else
{                              {
    --a;                           --a;
}                              }
```

The CPU fetches instructions sequentially, so we must tell the CPU that we want to skip some instructions if some condition is (not) met, for example, if a != 0.

B.NE (jump if not zero) and B.EQ (jump if zero) test the Z flag and change PC if the Z bit is cleared for B.NE or set for B.EQ. The following assembly language code is equivalent to the preceding C/C++ code:

```
        ADR  X0, A                        ADR  X0, A
        LDR  X1, [X0]                     LDR  X1, [X0]
        CMP  X1, #0                       TST  X1, X1
        B.NE label1                       B.EQ label1
        ADD  X0, X0, #1                   ADD  X0, X0, #1
        B  label2                         B    label2
label1: SUB  X0, X0, #1   label1: SUB  X0, X0, #1
label2: STR  X1, [X0]     label2: STR  X1, [X0]
```

Function Return Value

Many functions return values via the X0 register. For example:

```
long func();
```

The return value is in X0.

```
bool func();
```

The return value is in W0.

Bool values occupy one byte in memory, so the compiler uses W0 instead of X0.

Summary

In this chapter, we learned about CPU state flags, comparison instructions, conditional branches, and function return values – usually present in real binary code that we may need to disassemble to understand program logic during debugging.

The next chapter is our "graduating" project – we disassemble and analyze a project that uses function parameters which are pointers.

CHAPTER 13

Function Pointer Parameters

"FunctionPointerParameters" Project

It is our final project, and it can be downloaded from

github.com/apress/arm64-linux-debugging-disassembling-reversing/Chapter13/

A summary of the project source code:

```cpp
// FunctionParameters.cpp
int main(int argc, char* argv[])
{
    int a, b;

    printf("Enter a and b: ");
    scanf("%d %d", &a, &b);

    if (arithmetic (a, &b))
    {
        printf("Result = %d", b);
    }
}
```

© Dmitry Vostokov 2023

D. Vostokov, *Foundations of ARM64 Linux Debugging, Disassembling, and Reversing*,
https://doi.org/10.1007/978-1-4842-9082-8_13

153

```
        return 0;
}

// Arithmetic.cpp
bool arithmetic (int a, int *b)
{
        if (!b)
{
                return false;
        }

        *b = *b + a;
        ++a;
        *b = *b * a;

        return true;
}
```

Commented Disassembly

Here is the commented disassembly we get after compiling the project and loading it into GDB:

```
$ gcc FunctionParameters.cpp Arithmetic.cpp -o
FunctionParameters

$ gdb ./FunctionParameters
GNU gdb (GDB) Red Hat Enterprise Linux 7.6.1-120.0.2.el7
Copyright (C) 2013 Free Software Foundation, Inc.
License GPLv3+: GNU GPL version 3 or later <http://gnu.org/
licenses/gpl.html>
This is free software: you are free to change and
redistribute it.
```

There is NO WARRANTY, to the extent permitted by law. Type
"show copying"
and "show warranty" for details.
This GDB was configured as "aarch64-redhat-linux-gnu".
For bug reporting instructions, please see:
<http://www.gnu.org/software/gdb/bugs/>...
Reading symbols from /home/coredump/pflddr/A64/Chapter13/
FunctionParameters...(no debugging symbols found)...done.

(gdb) break main
Breakpoint 1 at 0x400660

(gdb) run
Starting program: /home/coredump/pflddr/A64/Chapter13/./
FunctionParameters

Breakpoint 1, 0x0000000000400660 in main ()
Missing separate debuginfos, use: debuginfo-install
glibc-2.17-325.0.2.el7_9.aarch64

(gdb) disas main
Dump of assembler code for function main:
```
   0x0000000000400658 <+0>:      stp     x29, x30, [sp,#-48]!
   0x000000000040065c <+4>:      mov     x29, sp
=> 0x0000000000400660 <+8>:      str     w0, [x29,#28]
   0x0000000000400664 <+12>:     str     x1, [x29,#16]
   0x0000000000400668 <+16>:     adrp    x0, 0x400000
   0x000000000040066c <+20>:     add     x0, x0, #0x7c0
   0x0000000000400670 <+24>:     bl      0x4004e0 <printf@plt>
   0x0000000000400674 <+28>:     adrp    x0, 0x400000
   0x0000000000400678 <+32>:     add     x0, x0, #0x7d0
   0x000000000040067c <+36>:     add     x1, x29, #0x2c
   0x0000000000400680 <+40>:     add     x2, x29, #0x28
```

```
   0x0000000000400684 <+44>:    bl      0x4004a0 <scanf@plt>
   0x0000000000400688 <+48>:    ldr     w0, [x29,#44]
   0x000000000040068c <+52>:    add     x1, x29, #0x28
   0x0000000000400690 <+56>:    bl      0x4006bc <_
                                         Z10arithmeticiPi>
   0x0000000000400694 <+60>:    uxtb    w0, w0
   0x0000000000400698 <+64>:    cmp     w0, wzr
   0x000000000040069c <+68>:    b.eq    0x4006b0 <main+88>
   0x00000000004006a0 <+72>:    ldr     w1, [x29,#40]
   0x00000000004006a4 <+76>:    adrp    x0, 0x400000
   0x00000000004006a8 <+80>:    add     x0, x0, #0x7d8
   0x00000000004006ac <+84>:    bl      0x4004e0 <printf@plt>
   0x00000000004006b0 <+88>:    mov     w0, #0x0             // #0
   0x00000000004006b4 <+92>:    ldp     x29, x30, [sp],#48
   0x00000000004006b8 <+96>:    ret
End of assembler dump.

(gdb) x/s 0x400000+0x7c0
0x4007c0:       "Enter a and b: "

(gdb) x/s 0x400000+0x7d0
0x4007d0:       "%d %d"

(gdb) x/s 0x400000+0x7d8
0x4007d8:       "Result = %d"

(gdb) disas arithmetic
Dump of assembler code for function _Z10arithmeticiPi:
   0x00000000004006bc <+0>:     sub     sp, sp, #0x10
   0x00000000004006c0 <+4>:     str     w0, [sp,#12]
   0x00000000004006c4 <+8>:     str     x1, [sp]
   0x00000000004006c8 <+12>:    ldr     x0, [sp]
```

```
0x00000000004006cc <+16>:     cmp      x0, xzr
0x00000000004006d0 <+20>:     b.ne     0x4006dc <_
                                        Z10arithmeticiPi+32>
0x00000000004006d4 <+24>:     mov      w0, #0x0              // #0
0x00000000004006d8 <+28>:     b        0x40071c <_
Z10arithmeticiPi+96>
0x00000000004006dc <+32>:     ldr      x0, [sp]
0x00000000004006e0 <+36>:     ldr      w1, [x0]
0x00000000004006e4 <+40>:     ldr      w0, [sp,#12]
0x00000000004006e8 <+44>:     add      w1, w1, w0
0x00000000004006ec <+48>:     ldr      x0, [sp]
0x00000000004006f0 <+52>:     str      w1, [x0]
0x00000000004006f4 <+56>:     ldr      w0, [sp,#12]
0x00000000004006f8 <+60>:     add      w0, w0, #0x1
0x00000000004006fc <+64>:     str      w0, [sp,#12]
0x0000000000400700 <+68>:     ldr      x0, [sp]
0x0000000000400704 <+72>:     ldr      w1, [x0]
0x0000000000400708 <+76>:     ldr      w0, [sp,#12]
0x000000000040070c <+80>:     mul      w1, w1, w0
0x0000000000400710 <+84>:     ldr      x0, [sp]
0x0000000000400714 <+88>:     str      w1, [x0]
0x0000000000400718 <+92>:     mov      w0, #0x1              // #1
0x000000000040071c <+96>:     add      sp, sp, #0x10
0x0000000000400720 <+100>:    ret
End of assembler dump.
```

main:

stp   x29, x30, [sp,#-48]!   **// establishing stack**
                                           frame for

mov	**x29, sp**	`//`	**parameters and local variables**
str	**w0, [x29,#28]**	`//`	**saving the first main parameter**
str	**x1, [x29,#16]**	`//`	**saving the second main parameter**
adrp	x0, 0x400000	`//`	the address of printf
add	x0, x0, #0x7c0	`//`	string parameter
bl	0x4004e0 <printf@plt>	`//`	printf("Enter a and b: ")
adrp	x0, 0x400000	`//`	the address of scanf
add	x0, x0, #0x7d0	`//`	string first parameter
add	x1, x29, #0x2c	`//`	the address of a relative to sp = x29
		`//`	scanf second parameter
add	x2, x29, #0x28	`//`	the address of b relative to sp = x29
		`//`	scanf third parameter
bl	0x4004a0 <scanf@plt>	`//`	scanf("%d %d", &a, &b)
ldr	w0, [x29,#44]	`//`	44=0x2c, w0 <- [a]
		`//`	arithmetic first parameter
add	x1, x29, #0x28	`//`	the address of b relative to sp = x29
		`//`	arithmetic second parameter
bl	0x4006bc <_Z10arithmeticiPi>	`//`	arithmetic (a, &b)

```
uxtb    w0, w0                  // zero-extends a byte
                                   result value to w0

cmp     w0, wzr                 // compares w0 with 0
                                //   wzr zero register
                                   always contains 0

b.eq    0x4006b0 <main+88>      // if equals zero goto
                                   function epilog

ldr     w1, [x29,#40]           // 40=0x28 w1 <- [b]
adrp    x0, 0x400000            // the address of printf
add     x0, x0, #0x7d8          //   string parameter
bl      0x4004e0 <printf@plt>   // printf("Result
                                   = %d", b)

0x00000000004006b0 <+88>:

mov     w0, #0x0                // main should return 0
ldp     x29, x30, [sp],#48      // restoring the
                                   previous stack frame

ret                             // return from main

arithmetic:

sub     sp, sp, #0x10           // establishing stack
                                   frame for
                                //   parameters and
                                   local variables

str     w0, [sp,#12]            // saving the first
                                   arithmetic
                                   parameter, p1

str     x1, [sp]                // saving the second
                                   arithmetic
                                   parameter, p2

ldr     x0, [sp]                // x0 <- [p2]
cmp     x0, xzr                 // if (x0 != 0)
```

```
b.ne      0x4006dc <_Z10arithmeticiPi+32>  // goto
0x00000000004006dc
mov       w0, #0x0                          // else { w0 <- 0,
                                                  return value
b         0x40071c <_Z10arithmeticiPi+96>  // goto epilog }
0x00000000004006dc <+32>:
ldr       x0, [sp]                          // x0 <- [p2]
ldr       w1, [x0]                          // x1 <- [x0], p2 is a
                                                  pointer, w1 <- *[p2]
ldr       w0, [sp,#12]                      // w0 <- [p1]
add       w1, w1, w0                        // w1 <- w1 + w0
ldr       x0, [sp]                          // x0 <- [p2]
str       w1, [x0]                          // [x0] <- w1,
                                                  *[p2] <- w1
ldr       w0, [sp,#12]                      // w0 <- [p1]
add       w0, w0, #0x1                      // w0 <- w0 + 1
str       w0, [sp,#12]                      // [p1] <- w0
ldr       x0, [sp]                          // x0 <- [p2]
ldr       w1, [x0]                          // 1 <- [x0], w1
                                                  <- *[p2]
ldr       w0, [sp,#12]                      // w0 <- [a]
mul       w1, w1, w0                        // w1 <- w1 + w0
ldr       x0, [sp]                          // x0 <- [p2]
str       w1, [x0]                          // [x0] <- w1,
                                                  *[p2] <- w1
mov       w0, #0x1                          // w0 <- 1,
                                                  return result

0x000000000040071c <+96>:
add       sp, sp, #0x10                     // restoring the
                                                  previous stack frame
ret                                         // return from
                                                  arithmetic
```

Summary

In this chapter, we disassembled and analyzed a project that used function parameters which are pointers.

The next, final chapter of the book summarizes various basic disassembly patterns.

CHAPTER 14

Summary of Code Disassembly Patterns

This final chapter summarizes the various patterns we have encountered during the reading of this book.

Function Prolog/Epilog

Function prolog

```
stp   x29, x30, [sp,#-48]!
mov   x29, sp
```

Some code may omit `stp` if there are no nested calls inside:

```
sub   sp, sp, #0x10
```

Function epilog

```
ldp   x29, x30, [sp],#48
ret
```

Some code may omit to restore X29/X30 if there are no nested calls inside:

```
add   sp, sp, #0x10
ret
```

© Dmitry Vostokov 2023
D. Vostokov, *Foundations of ARM64 Linux Debugging, Disassembling, and Reversing*,
https://doi.org/10.1007/978-1-4842-9082-8_14

Knowing the prolog can help identify situations when symbol files or function start addresses are not correct. For example, suppose we have the following backtrace:

```
foo3+0x5F
foo2+0x8F
foo+0x20
```

If we disassemble the *foo2* function and see that it does not start with the prolog, we may assume that backtrace needs more attention:

```
(gdb) x/i foo2
0x0000000000455165:    ldr    x0, [x1]
```

ADR (Address)

The following instructions

```
adrp x0, 0x400000
add  x0, x0, #0x7d0
```

are equivalent to the following instruction for smaller addresses:

```
adr  x0, 0x4007d0
```

Passing Parameters

The first eight function parameters are passed from left to right via

```
X0 - X7
```

Note   Although we haven't seen examples for more than eight function parameters, they are passed via the stack, for example, via STR or STP instructions. Passed parameters are saved on the stack by the callee.

Static/global variable address (or string constant)

```
adrp x0, 0x400000
add  x0, x0, #0x7d0
```

Local variable value

```
ldr  x0, [reg]          // local variable value
call func
```

Local variable address

```
add  x0, x29, #offset    // local variable address
call func
```

Accessing Saved Parameters and Local Variables

Local word (int) variable value

```
ldr  w0, [sp, #offset]
```

Local doubleword (long) variable value

```
ldr  x0, [sp, #offset]
```

Local variable address

```
add  x0, sp, #offset
```

Dereferencing a pointer to a doubleword value

```
ldr  x0, [sp, #offset]
ldr  x1, [x0]
```

Dereferencing a pointer to a word value

```
ldr  x0, [sp, #offset]
ldr  w1, [x0]
```

Optimized code may not use stack locations to address function parameters (use only registers through which the parameters were passed) as can be seen in the previous chapter's example compiled with the -O2 switch:

```
(gdb) disas arithmetic(int, int*)
Dump of assembler code for function _Z10arithmeticiPi:
   0x00000000004006b0 <+0>:     cbz    x1, 0x4006d0
                                        <_Z10arithmeticiPi+32>
   0x00000000004006b4 <+4>:     ldr    w2, [x1]
   0x00000000004006b8 <+8>:     add    w3, w0, #0x1
   0x00000000004006bc <+12>:    add    w0, w0, w2
   0x00000000004006c0 <+16>:    mul    w0, w0, w3
   0x00000000004006c4 <+20>:    str    w0, [x1]
   0x00000000004006c8 <+24>:    mov    w0, #0x1            // #1
   0x00000000004006cc <+28>:    ret
   0x00000000004006d0 <+32>:    mov    w0, w1
   0x00000000004006d4 <+36>:    ret
End of assembler dump.
```

Summary

This chapter can be used as a reference to basic disassembly patterns.

Index

A

Access violation, 70
ADD, 5, 9, 10, 13–15, 47, 151
Address (ADR), 7, 9, 10, 13, 16, 17,
        78, 79, 164
Address of another memory cell,
        35, 65, 71
ADDS, 147
ADRP, 9, 164
AND, 90, 148
Application Binary Interface (ABI)
        mismatch problem, 144
Application crash, 70
Arithmetic, 139
Arithmetic Project, 3, 19
Array elements, 124
Assembly code, 21, 25, 28
Assignment, 6

B

B, 114, 151
Base pointer, 124
B.EQ, 151
Binary notation, 32
Binary representation, 31
BL, 110

BL/BRL, 115, 116
B.NE, 151
BR, 115
Break command, 75
Breakpoint, 22, 41, 75, 95, 119,
        130, 141
bt command, 121
Byte, 60

C

Callee, 116, 135, 144
Caller, 116, 117, 129, 144
CMP, 148–150
Code reconstruction, 95
Commented disassembly, 154
Compiler optimization, 28
Computer memory, 1
Computer program, 5
Conditional jumps, 151
Contents at the memory
        address, 4, 36
Continue command, 120

D

Dangling pointer, 70
.data, 72, 93

Printed in the United States
by Baker & Taylor Publisher Services